D0272892

SUBMARINE

German Knight
Cross medal

Russian submarine
commander's cap

US submarine
commander's
uniform

Submarine from
Thunderbirds
television series

Bridge binoculars

Manned
submersible

NAUTILE

World War II
British Unity-Class
submarine model

US submarine
shoulder patch

DK EYEWITNESS GUIDES

US submarine
shoulder patch

SUBMARINE

Written by
NEIL MALLARD

In association with
THE ROYAL NAVY SUBMARINE MUSEUM

German U-boat
pressure gauge

Model of
Garrett's *Resurgam*

Soviet Navy
submarine pennant

Model of Russian
Oscar-Class
submarine

Model of World War I
British Unity-Class
submarine

German Enigma
coding machine

US submarine
shoulder patch

German submarine
escape breathing
apparatus

DK

LONDON, NEW YORK,
MELBOURNE, MUNICH, AND DELHI

Editor Andrea Mills
Designers Tim Brown, Ann Cannings
Project editor Giles Sparrow
Senior editor Kitty Blount
Managing editor Linda Esposito
Managing art editor Jane Thomas
Digital artwork Robin Hunter
Production controller Erica Rosen
Special photography Andy Crawford, Steve Tanner
Picture researchers Sean Hunter, Harriet Mills
Picture librarians Sarah Mills, Karl Stange, Gemma Woodward
DTP designer Siu Yin Ho
Jacket designer Chris Drew

Consultant
Commander J.J.Tall, OBE RN
Director of the Royal Navy Submarine Museum

This Eyewitness ® Guide has been conceived by
Dorling Kindersley Limited and Editions Gallimard

First published in Great Britain in 2003 by
Dorling Kindersley Limited
80 Strand, London WC2R 0RL

A CIP catalogue record for this book is
available from the British Library.

ISBN 0-7513-6781-8

Colour reproduction by Colourscan, Singapore
Printed in China by Toppan Printing Co., (Shenzhen) Ltd.

See our complete
catalogue at

www.dk.com

Contents

British Resolution-Class submarine patch

What is a submarine?

A SUBMARINE IS AN underwater craft whose invention revolutionized war at sea and which has enabled humans to explore the hidden world beneath the ocean surface. Submarines range in size from a small car to giant vessels twice the size of a jumbo jet. Their shape, method of propulsion, and function also vary widely. Submersibles are designed to undertake short journeys, while nuclear-powered subs can travel around the world without stopping. Specialized vessels can go to great depths to conduct research. They are lowered by a wire from a mother ship. Submarines are also used for fun. These pleasure submarines allow tourists to view underwater life.

U-BOAT
In both world wars, the U-boat was one of Germany's most feared weapons. Ranging far and wide throughout the world's shipping lanes, U-boats gave Germany its best hope of starving out the British through sinking their merchant ships carrying supplies. Eventually, the U-boats were beaten by the convoy system and the combined forces of aircraft and surface warships.

SUBMARINE "EYES"
The periscope allows a submarine to peek at the outside world with little chance of being seen itself. Most submarines have two periscopes, one with a wide angle for searching an expanse of open ocean and the other a thin tube for attacking at close range. By a flick of a handle, the submarine captain can magnify a target up to six times, making it easier to identify and attack.

SUBMARINE ATTACK
During the two world wars, millions of tonnes of shipping fell victim to the submarines of both sides. Submarines were able to use their cloak of invisibility unchallenged for many years, until technology provided the hunters with radar in aircraft and ASDIC (sonar) in ships. This sequence of photographs taken through a submarine periscope in World War II shows a destroyer sinking after receiving a direct hit from a torpedo.

In 1915, a shot fired by a Turkish gunboat managed to hit this periscope belonging to a British submarine.

"It is possible to make a shippe or boate that may goe under the water to the bottom, and so come up again at your pleasure."

WILLIAM BOURNE
1578

NUCLEAR SUBMARINE

The introduction of nuclear power into submarines led to another revolution in naval warfare. Unlike the relatively slow diesel-electric submarines, nuclear-powered subs could travel faster than their selected targets. In addition, because a nuclear reactor does not need oxygen, the submarines rarely had to visit the surface and could stay on patrol for months rather than weeks. Due to their unlimited power, nuclear-powered submarines could also be built large enough to carry huge intercontinental ballistic missiles.

SUBMERSIBLE

Today, submersibles are used for a wide variety of tasks, from underwater search-and-rescue missions to surveying the sea bed and repairing oil rigs or telecommunications cables. Built in Finland and operated by Russian scientists, *Mir I* (pictured above) and *Mir II* were launched in 1987. They are among a number of submersibles capable of diving to more than 6,100 m (20,000 ft)

US Navy diver descending to enter the submarine

TOURIST SUB

The first tourist submarine emerged from a craft designed by Frenchman Claude Goubet in 1899 (p. 16), which was eventually sold to a Swiss businessman and used for voyages under Lake Geneva. Submarine tourism took off after World War II, with the construction of a wide range of craft with capacities of up to 64 people. These operate mainly in the Caribbean and off the coast of Florida.

The clear waters of the Caribbean provide a great view for tourists

LIFE ON BOARD

Submariners do not expect to enjoy the luxuries of a surface ship, particularly being able to move about freely and breathe fresh air. Comradeship goes a long way to make up for living in cramped conditions. Here, crewmen on a nuclear submarine enjoy a game of cards. Once it was impossible even to wash, let alone shower, and food came mainly from tins. Conditions are much more comfortable today, although teamwork is still vital.

How a submarine works

IN THE SAME WAY that an iceberg is mostly hidden underwater, there is much more to a submarine than is visible on the surface. The narrow deck rests on top of a rounded hull that bulges outwards and which is divided into an inner and outer section. Between the sections are ballast tanks that are filled with seawater to submerge the submarine, then they are blown dry with compressed air to bring the boat back to the surface. The physics of "ballasting" was first suggested in 1578 by an English gunner, William Bourne, and the process was perfected in the late 19th century. An engine drives one or more propellers at the stern (rear) to push the submarine through the water (pp. 10–11), the rudder allows it to steer, and wing-like hydroplanes keep the submarine level or change its depth.

One of two propellers

After hydroplanes for depth control

Conning tower and mast

Ballast tanks attached to hull

Vent for ballast tanks

Forward hydroplanes

A CLASSIC SUBMARINE
The British D-Class, launched in 1908–11, was a major step forward in submarine design. Larger than previous models, these 550-tonne submarines were also among the first to use diesel engines. They had saddle tanks for ballast and a top surface speed of 14 knots.

Ventilation intake

Casing for crew to walk on

BALLAST TANKS
Objects float or sink in water according to how dense they are. Filling ballast tanks with water enables a submarine to increase its density. To dive, the air is allowed to escape through vents, and the ballast tanks fill with water. The sub sinks until it "hovers" underwater, and maintains this neutral buoyancy through the use of internal trim tanks. To surface again, high-pressure air forces the water out.

1. Submarine with ballast tanks full of air

2. Vents open and water enters tanks, forcing out the air.

3. Submarine sinks until it "floats" underwater.

4. Air is blown into tanks to force out the water.

5. Submarine rises.

6. Fully buoyant submarine reaches the surface.

MANOEUVRABILITY
Modern nuclear submarines are capable of rapid manoeuvres that would tear a more traditional submarine apart. This photograph shows a USN Los Angeles-Class submarine performing an emergency surfacing exercise. The submarine blows its ballast tanks with high-pressure air, tilts its hydroplanes to point it sharply upwards, and propels at maximum speed. The submarine had to take care not to leap clear of the water!

WINGS UNDER WATER
Beneath the surface,
a submarine changes depth
by using its hydroplanes.
These are underwater
"wings" that can pivot to
change the amount of
water resistance they
encounter. A modern
submarine virtually "flies"
through the water and can
manoeuvre in combat like
a slow-motion jet fighter.

Bow

Rescue hatch

Forward hydroplanes

Streamlined conning tower

Russian Akula-Class submarine

PERFECT DIVE
In a perfectly controlled dive, a
submarine sinks gracefully below the
waves without tipping anyone out of
his bunk! As the ballast tanks flood,
the submarine stays horizontal,
becomes heavier, and sinks.

CRASH DIVE
During wartime, a submarine could "crash dive"
in 30 seconds. This move was necessary if under
threat from an aircraft. A submarine would
increase its weight by filling its ballast tanks
and flooding water into its internal trim
tanks. This submarine is "venting" air to
go underwater. However, it will remain
vulnerable to attack for several minutes
due to the tell-tale "swirl" it leaves on
the surface of the sea.

Rudder for steering

Propeller

After hydroplane

THE STERN
Conventional submarines had a diesel engine and an
electric motor on each side of the hull. Spinning drive
shafts linked the engines and motors to two
propellers, immediately in front of the rudder used
for steering. A horizontal guard around the stern
prevented ropes or debris from fouling the propellers.

Submarine propulsion

For thousands of years, ships of all sizes had been driven by the wind or paddles. Wind-power was an impossibility for submarines, and so at first the only option was to use oars. During the 1700s, the invention of the screw propeller enabled progress to be made in submarine design, but it still relied on human muscle power. Mechanisms such as clockwork, steam engines, and electrical motors all emerged during the 19th century. However, the major breakthrough was the internal combustion engine linked to a battery. Highly volatile gasoline was the only fuel available in the early days, but this gradually gave way to safer fuels such as paraffin and diesel.

Type XXI
U-boat

*Crew member
operating rudder*

*Commander in charge
of speed and direction*

*Operator of the
anti-ship ram*

Anti-ship ram

Propeller   *Crankshaft*

HUMAN POWER
The American Civil War produced many submarine designs from both sides. A Union submarine, *Alligator*, built in 1862 by the French diver and designer Brutus de Villeroi, was powered by 16 men turning a crankshaft that then turned a propeller. The hull contained only limited air, so it had a very small radius of action.

*Gustave Zédé
submarine*

*Collapsible bridge to keep
crew clear of water*

STORING POWER
French designer Gustave Zédé concentrated his efforts on electric power, and on completion the submarine carrying his name carried 360 electric batteries. This craft was also fitted with hydroplanes for greater control. In 1899, it carried out a successful dummy attack on a French battleship.

*Inside the engine room
of a World War I U-boat*

THE ENGINE ROOM
In diesel-electric submarines, the crew had to learn to live with a combination of engine noise when on the surface and the ever-present smell of diesel fuel when submerged. Officers and their men worked in very cramped conditions with minimal facilities during cruises that could last many days.

*Smooth shape
to avoid noise*

SILENT RUNNING
The propeller's size and shape have changed over the years. A turning propeller can be heard by the enemy, so modifications have been introduced to make it run more quietly. Boats have used up to three propellers, but today most submarines have one large "prop".

Streamlined conning tower

THE DIESEL-ELECTRIC

By World War II, all submarines afloat used diesel-electric propulsion, and the German Type XXI, which appeared in 1944, was the most streamlined design of this type. By coupling the diesel unit to a generator, the submarine could recharge its batteries while on the surface and then switch to electric power when submerged. The Type XX1 had a cruising range of 24,000 km (15,000 miles) – enough to enable it to reach Japan.

More blades for greater acceleration

British Navy Hydrogen Peroxide boat

WALTHER BOAT

The German "Walther Boat" used Hydrogen Peroxide to drive a turbine, producing an underwater speed in excess of 20 knots. Fuel consumption proved very high, however, and so the cruise range at top speed was limited to just 128 km (80 miles). The British Navy continued to experiment with this fuel after the war, but later abandoned the project in favour of nuclear power.

Propeller securing nut

Officer and lookout on the bridge

USSN Los Angeles-Class at speed

Propeller blades accelerate water behind them and create thrust

NUCLEAR PROPULSION

Theoretically, nuclear power gives a submarine unlimited range and underwater endurance, so the main limiting factor on the length of time spent at sea is the amount of food that can be carried for the crew. The heat provided by the reactor is used to boil water, and the resultant steam is used to turn a main engine driving through a clutch onto a shaft, at the end of which is a propeller.

Early dreams and designs

THE DESIRE TO EXPLORE the ocean depths was the motivation for early pioneers of the submarine. As with so many scientific advances, these designers knew little of the problems that lay ahead. The most obvious challenge was how to make the craft sink and then rise again. Beyond that were the problems of maintaining an air supply inside the craft, driving it under water when the propeller had not yet been invented, and ensuring water did not seep in. The squeezing effect of water pressure even at quite shallow depths and the difference in density between fresh and sea water were two further considerations. As more was learned from experiments, the submarine design we know today began to emerge.

ALEXANDER – THE GREAT DIVER
In 342 BC, Alexander the Great decided to look at what lay under the waters of his empire, so he had a glass diving bell constructed. Legend has it that he, a monkey, and a cockerel entered through a hatch that could be fastened by chains. Then they were all lowered by a long rope to the sea floor, where they had a picnic lunch.

BALLAST BASICS
In 1547, Englishman William Bourne worked out the basic principle of all submarines. To make a boat sink, you had to increase its weight by filling ballast tanks with water. To make it surface again, you pumped the water out. He placed a hollow mast above the water to supply fresh air.

Screw-controlled ballast tanks

Bourne's wooden-hulled design

DA VINCI'S EXPERIMENTS
Leonardo da Vinci (1452–1519) designed an early breathing apparatus. It failed because the proposed breathing tube was more than twice as long as the human windpipe, and so the tube would soon have been dangerously full of carbon dioxide. The tube would need to be short enough to empty completely with a single breath.

Hollow tube

Tie-on mouthpiece

NATURE'S SUBMARINE
Nautilus is the most common name for a submarine. It comes from nature's own submarine, the *Nautilus Popilius*. This sea creature lives within the outer shell of its home. To rise and fall, it pumps out water with gas generated from the inner shells.

BORELLI'S BOAT
In the 1670s, Italian scientist Giovanni Borelli discovered that a fish controls its depth by varying the weight of water carried in its bladder. Using goatskin bladders for ballast tanks, he planned a boat with levers to flood and empty the tanks. He included oars to act like a fish tail and move his boat through the water.

VAN DREBBEL'S ODYSSEY
In 1620, Dutch scientist Cornelius van Drebbel demonstrated to England's King James his oar-driven submersible in a four-mile voyage between Westminster and Greenwich on the River Thames in London. Diaries of the period describe his vessel as an enclosed rowboat with waterproof leather oars. Its hydrodynamic form pulled it under water when it was propelled ahead by the oarsmen, proving that shape was crucial to submarine design.

FACT OR FICTION?
As the inventors explored the depths, the fiction writers followed. The most successful was 19th-century writer Jules Verne. His *20,000 Leagues under the Sea* (an impossible calculation as the ocean is not this deep) follows the adventures of a submarine crew. Much of the fiction would later become fact.

WIND UP
During the Anglo-Dutch War of 1652–54, Frenchman De Son built a submersible with a clockwork engine for the Dutch. Once it was wound up, it was meant to travel for eight hours, but when the submersible was tested, the paddlewheels failed to go round because of water resistance and the idea was abandoned.

Propulsion by paddlewheel

Battering ram made this the first underwater warship in history

Blockade busters

A NAVAL BLOCKADE is established by a group of ships patrolling off a harbour or bay to prevent defending ships from being able to leave or enter. It is the maritime equivalent of laying siege to a castle and starving the opposition into surrender. This tactic was used on many occasions by the superpowers of the 18th century, the French and British, who had numerous powerful wooden warships. In 1776, during the American War of Independence (1775–83), a tiny submersible dared to challenge the might of British blockaders off the New York Harbour. It conducted the first submerged attack in history.

Diving propeller for up-and-down movement

Brass cover with six portholes

Reinforced wooden bodywork

Forward movement propeller

Foot pedals to turn the propeller

BUSHNELL'S TURTLE
Designed by the American David Bushnell, the *Turtle* required a strong and multi-talented operator. The pilot had to navigate, steer, and operate the control pedals with his feet to turn the horizontal propeller. Once close to the target, he had to dive underneath it using the downward propeller. The idea was to screw a limpet mine into the enemy's hull, and then escape before it exploded!

THE TURTLE ATTACKS
In 1776, Sergeant Ezra Lee piloted the *Turtle* underneath the flagship of the British blockading ships, HMS *Eagle*. But he unfortunately tried to screw his mine onto a metal section of the hull. After an exhausting 30 minutes, Lee gave up and fled.

FULTON'S NAUTILUS

The American engineer Robert Fulton (1765–1815) designed an all-metal submarine, *Nautilus*, which was powered on the surface by a sail. In 1800, he demonstrated his design to Napoleon. The French Emperor was so impressed by what he saw that he paid Fulton a large sum of money to develop his craft. Sadly for Fulton, Napoleon abandoned his plans to invade Britain and attacked Russia instead, so *Nautilus* never went to war.

Collapsible sail

Propeller

Space for crew

Anchor

Spar torpedo with exploding charge at tip

Access hatch

TUBE CRAFT

During the American Civil War (1861–1865), the North had a blockading stranglehold on Confederate forces in Charleston, South Carolina. In desperation, Horace Hunley converted a boiler tube into a submersible craft with a spar torpedo as a weapon. Sea trials for the unwieldy submarine were a disaster, and a total of 23 sailors, including Hunley, were drowned. But history was made in 1864 when CSS *Hunley* attacked and sank the Union frigate *Housatonic*.

Hand-cranked propeller

INTELLIGENT WHALE

A top secret American Civil War design for the Union forces of the North under Abraham Lincoln, *Intelligent Whale* was powered by six men turning the propeller cranks. It was produced to add underwater strength to the Union ships blockading the Confederate ports. After several crewmen were drowned during trials, the craft did not survive to see active service.

The 30-tonne *Brandtaucher* now on display in a Munich museum

U-BOAT ANCESTOR

When Danish warships blockaded Schleswig-Holstein in north Germany in the 1850s, the Bavarian officer Wilhelm Bauer took the first steps to create what was to become the formidable German submarine fleet. His first design, *Der Brandtaucher*, promptly sank twice. But Bauer and his crew became heroes for being the first to escape from a submarine underwater.

The true submarine is born

By the late 1800s, inventors were working to develop submarines that were practical. None of the earlier designs could be controlled effectively underwater, nor could they be propelled without using human muscle power. The man who finally overcame these problems was Irish-born American John Philip Holland (1841–1914). Around this time, Englishman Robert Whitehead invented the locomotive torpedo, intended at first for use in surface warships. The combination of submarines and torpedoes produced the most lethal development in naval history.

ELECTRIC POWER
In 1885, Frenchman Claude Goubet built the world's first successful electrically propelled submarine. His electrical accumulators stored the power and, when clumped together, they made a battery. One of Goubet's craft remained on the bottom of Cherbourg Harbour, France, for a record-breaking eight hours. However, the design was too awkward to be a lasting success.

Steam funnel

Flattened front for easy diving

Entrance hatch

Possibly the only lifeboat ever carried on a submarine

STEAM POWER
British Reverend George W. Garrett designed one of the first steam-powered submarines – *Resurgam*. While underwater, the boiler was doused, and steam for turning the propeller was stored in pressurized tanks. The same system was used to turn the wheels of the first London Underground trains. *Resurgam*, meaning "I shall rise again", failed to live up to her name because she sank under tow in 1880.

Garrett and his young son join the captain and engineer on the recently completed Resurgam in 1879.

Cut-away model of Resurgam

Conning tower in style of diver's helmet

SHARED IDEAS
Undeterred by the failure of *Resurgam*, Garrett shared the idea of his steam-powered submarine with Swede Thorsten Nordenfeldt, the inventor of the machine gun. The first of the Nordenfeldts (above) was produced in 1883. Diving was achieved by two downward propellers. This larger and longer design also failed, as little control was possible. Garrett died penniless.

Steam furnace

Oak planking over the central hull

Steam-powered engine

FIRST SUB
The British Royal Navy's first submarine, *Holland I*, joined the fleet in 1901, and is seen here off Portsmouth. The submarine was powered on the surface by a petrol engine, which operated a generator to charge electric batteries. Once submerged, the engine was stopped and the batteries powered the boat.

JOHN PHILIP HOLLAND
Hailed as the "father of the modern submarine", John Philip Holland is seen here emerging from *Holland VI* in April 1898. He emigrated from Ireland to the United States, where he began his landmark work. His designs were later adopted by the navies of Britain, Japan, Russia, and Sweden.

> *"The submarine is the coming type of war vessel for sea fighting."*
>
> ADMIRAL OF THE FLEET, LORD FISHER
> May 1913

Explosive charge inside nose cone

Propeller

THE TORPEDO
In 1868, the British engineer Robert Whitehead designed and built the first self-propelled torpedo. Powered by compressed air, it was 4.8 m (16 ft) long and carried a 34-kg (76-lb) charge of guncotton to a range of more than 300 m (980 ft). The torpedo, nicknamed the "Devil's Device", was soon used in battle, and for a while it was preferred over the gun as a ship's main armament.

1.5 m- (5 ft-) diameter propeller

Conning tower

Ventilation masts

Innovative casing for crew to walk on

Whale-shaped body

WHALE–SHAPED SUB
Holland built submarines for the US Navy, with the first entering service in 1900. Whale-shaped USS *Holland* had three torpedoes to be fired from a 46-cm (18-in) torpedo tube, and a mortar for surface use. Successors to this design sank thousands of ships.

Subs go to war

W~ORLD WAR~ I (1914–18) was the first real submarine war. Germany soon realized that sinking merchant ships bringing food supplies to France and Britain gave them the chance to win a "starvation war". Under international law, submarines had to stop and search a target for prohibited goods before sinking it. But faced with the British blockade, the Germans sank ships without warning. Outraged, the United States joined the war in 1917, and, at last, the convoy system was introduced to enable huge fleets of supply ships to travel in relative safety. Despite earlier success against unarmed ships, the U-boats failed to win the battle.

THE U-BOATS ARE OUT!
In 1914, Germany entered the war with just 20 U-boats. U-boat imagery was widely used for propaganda by the German government to show the destructive capability of the submarine and Germany's military strength.

SHIPPING LOSSES
By the end of the war, German submarines had sunk 5,554 merchant ships. The U-boats also suffered, though. From a total of 372 submarines, they lost 178, most of them sunk by mines. Despite these huge losses, the submarine had proved itself as one of the most decisive weapons of naval power.

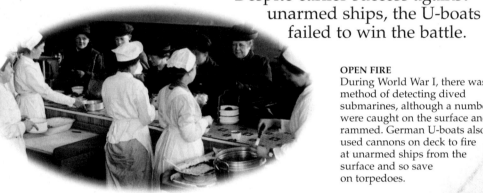

OPEN FIRE
During World War I, there was no method of detecting dived submarines, although a number were caught on the surface and rammed. German U-boats also used cannons on deck to fire at unarmed ships from the surface and so save on torpedoes.

FOOD SHORTAGES
By the middle of 1917, the Royal Navy was struggling to keep the supply routes to Britain open due to constant attacks by U-boats. The government was forced to introduce food rationing and even communal kitchens in order to control the food shortage.

U-boat crew fire a deck cannon to stop an enemy steamer.

SIMPLICISSIMUS

A German cartoon mocking US calls to halt attacks on passenger ships

Lusitania took only 20 minutes to sink.

REIGNING IN THE U-BOATS

German tactics were to target all Allied shipping, including passenger ships. In March 1917, three American vessels went down. Two days later the United States declared war on Germany. By October 1918, Germany was desperate for peace, and on October 20th, the attacks on passenger ships ended.

Net-cutter to break through underwater obstructions

10-cm (4-in) gun for surface action

Minelaying U-boat *UC5*

LOSS OF A LINER

The tide of American public opinion had turned against Germany quite early in the war when the Cunard passenger liner *Lusitania* fell victim to the *U-20* off the Irish coast in May 1915. Of the 1,198 passengers and crew who died, 128 were Americans. The United States was shocked by these deaths, and the anti-war lobby was weakened.

Mine launching area at stern

Conning tower

MINELAYERS

Both sides used submarines as minelayers. Boats laid these "explosive eggs" to go off without warning and take many victims. Some U-boats were adapted to lay mines and then lure warships to them – a tactic that led sailors to call them "Judas Boats". But minelaying was a dangerous business, as the minelayer itself risked being blown up.

"The submarine is the most formidable thing the war has produced – by far."

US AMBASSADOR WALTER PAGE
1917

Doomed designs

BETWEEN THE WARS, many new submarines were developed, most of which failed – often costing lives in the process. These were experimental years, with inventors pushing boundaries to use submarines in different ways. Most were aiming to increase the effectiveness and range of submarines. Although many of the designs showed brilliance in tactical thought, the submarines turned out to be disappointing or even disastrous. Submarine designers learned from their mistakes and began to plan a new generation of submarines.

SUBMARINE ON WHEELS
It was easy to recognize a submarine designed by the American Simon Lake (1866–1945) – it was fitted with wheels. Lake was a great believer in the working qualities of the submarine, so he wanted to make use of the sea floor by allowing his submarines to bump their way along the bottom. Although Lake's designs were always innovative, they never caught on.

K-CLASS
The steam-driven K-Class was introduced into the British Royal Navy in 1916 as a fleet escort and continued in service until the 1920s. Even though they could reach high speeds, they were extremely clumsy submarines and suffered many mishaps – so many that they became known as the "Kalamitous Ks". *K4* (above) was involved in an accident, as were eight other K-Class submarines.

Communications mast

Periscope

Four torpedo tubes for attack

Lift for carrying ammunition to gun

Breach for loading shells

The crew of Surcouf *line up for a ceremonial entry into harbour.*

GIANT SUBMARINE

Launched in 1929, the bulky French *Surcouf* was a one-off design. With a crew of 150, *Surcouf* had ten torpedo tubes and two guns similar to those carried on large warships for surface action. It was these innovations and her gigantic size that proved her downfall. Too complicated, she was a bigger threat to herself than the enemy and was finally sunk in a collision during World War II.

Built-up conning tower to see over hangar

Crane for retrieving seaplane

Hangar

Parnell Peto seaplane

AIRCRAFT CARRIER

The idea behind carrying an aircraft on a submarine was sensible in theory. The submarine could operate ahead of a group of battleships without being seen by the enemy, pop up to the surface, quickly launch its aircraft, recover the aircraft on completion of its mission, and dive again. But the theory proved hard to put into practice – HMS *M2* sank in 1932 during an exercise off southern England when water flooded into the hangar.

CRUISER SUBMARINE

The British Admiralty commissioned the cruiser submarine in 1923. The largest sub in the world, *X1* had more powerful deck guns than a surface ship. The Washington Treaty limited the submarine tonnage that each country could build, which meant the heavy *X1* was scrapped in 1937 to make way for three more conventional U-class submarines.

Multiple deck guns

Main barrel (30 cm (12 in) in diameter)

Painted hull to camouflage the vessel

THE BIG GUN

During World War I, not one ship was sunk by a torpedo outside a range of 914 m (3,000 ft). The idea behind the design of the M-Class was to attach an old battleship gun that was capable of sinking a warship at ten times this range. This design was abandoned in 1925 when HMS *M1* was run down by a merchant ship during a firing exercise.

World War II

WORLD WAR II (1939–45) brought together the destructive capability of the German U-boats in the Atlantic and of their American equivalents in the Pacific. The result was the loss of millions of tonnes of merchant shipping, including the almost total destruction of the Japanese merchant fleet. In the Atlantic, following major fleet losses in the early years, the war swung against the U-boat. Germany fell behind in the technical race, and there were many more Allied warships and radar-fitted aircraft than U-boats. By 1943, the U-boats became the hunted rather than the hunters. Now called "iron coffins" by crews who would expect to survive no more than three trips, 785 boats were sunk in World War II. Eight out of ten submariners died in action.

GRAND ADMIRAL DONITZ
A U-boat commander in World War I, Karl Donitz went on to mastermind the U-boat campaign in World War II. He started the "wolf pack" system that saw up to 20 submarines attack a single convoy. He briefly succeeded Adolf Hitler in the last weeks of the war.

Attack periscope

U-boat emblem

Conning tower

Communications aerial

Anti-shipping gun

Four torpedo tubes

TYPE IX U-BOAT
During World War II, a larger version of the Type VII U-boat arrived. The "Nines" acted as attack craft, blockade runners, and "milch cows" – supply ships for wolf packs on extended operations in the Atlantic and Indian oceans.

Forward torpedo room and crew's quarters

Hydrophone room

Radio room

"The only thing that ever really frightened me during the war was the U-boat peril."
PRIME MINISTER WINSTON CHURCHILL

MASS PRODUCTION
The Germans, British, and Americans recognized that large submarine fleets were essential. For Germany, the excellent Type VIIs proved to be the workhorse in the Atlantic, the British S-, T-, and U-Classes fought with distinction in the Mediterranean, and the US Gato- and Balao-Classes dominated the Pacific.

Deck gun for use against small targets

Radar mast

HIGH SPEED SUB
Before it entered World War II, the US ordered 73 Gato-Class submarines. These high-speed vessels were equipped with a very effective radar and formed the backbone of the US submarine effort. Although they made up only 3 per cent of the US naval force, they sank more than half of the Japanese total tonnage lost.

A SINKING IN THE PACIFIC
One of five American aircraft carriers lost in the Pacific, the USS *Wasp* was the only one to fall victim to a Japanese submarine. She was hit off Guadalcanal in September 1942, by two torpedoes from a spread of four. The other two torpedoes went on to damage the battleship *North Carolina* and blow the bows off the destroyer *O'Brien*.

Black smoke billows from torpedoed USS Wasp.

Anti-aircraft gun

Officers' quarters

Engine room

Rear torpedo tubes

Rudder

Electric motor for running underwater

Propeller

Batteries for storing power

Electrical panel operator

U-BOAT SINKING
The veteran American coastguard cutter *Spencer* attacked Type IX U-boat U175 in April 1943 in the North Atlantic. The crew watched their depth charges explode before they rescued 42 of the 54 U-boat crew. The U-boat had failed to break up a large Allied convoy.

The trophy for HMS *Tiptoe*

LAST DANCE
All Royal Navy submarines have a "trophy". HMS *Tiptoe* not only had a ballet dancer on her badge, but also carried a pair of ballet shoes worn by famous ballerina Moira Shearer. *Tiptoe* was the last submarine to sink an enemy ship in World War II. In August 1945, she launched a torpedo that sank a Japanese freighter.

Mini-submarines

Large submarines could not penetrate well-protected harbours, so they had to extend their capability by other means. The Italians were first to come up with the idea of "human torpedoes" – an electrically propelled craft driven by frogmen that would be carried close to a target by a "mother" submarine. Their range was limited, so the British and the Japanese developed the idea and built mini-submarines with a longer range and a bigger punch. Mini-submarines enjoyed some success during World War II, although it was a one-way mission for many.

Helmet with mask and breathing apparatus

Italian chariot

UNDERWATER CHARIOT
The first use of the human torpedo was during World War I. The Italian Navy resurrected the idea during the 1930s when a team of engineers converted a standard torpedo into a chariot on which two men rode. The two-man crew were dressed as frogmen, and could dive their craft as deep as 9 m (30 ft) to get under defensive nets. It was dangerous and exhausting work. The Italians called their craft Maiale (pigs); the British equivalent was the "chariot".

CHARIOTEER'S HELMET
The crews of the first "chariots" had to make do with gear that was adapted from submarine escape equipment. Later, special equipment like this helmet was developed.

Net cutters

British Mk1 Chariot

THE X-CRAFT
Designed by a World War I submariner, the X-craft was a perfect submarine in miniature. It lacked the range to travel long distances, so it had to be towed to the target area by a "mother" submarine. It was used in a number of operations – cutting subsurface telephone cables in the Far East, landing special forces in France, and leading in the Allied invasion force on D-Day. Its renowned exploits were the crippling of the German battleship *Tirpitz* and the Japanese cruiser *Takao*.

CUTTING THROUGH THE DEFENCES
Anti-submarine nets were used in both world wars to try to stop submarines getting through or attacking with torpedoes. These nets were hung across harbour entrances or around possible targets. Net cutters were soon developed to hack through them. Here the crew of a British Mk1 Chariot prepare to cut their way through a harbour net.

The only way that the X-craft commander could remain on deck was by strapping himself to a special rail.

X-craft under tow

HAWAII FAILURE
As Japanese aircraft swarmed over the US Pacific fleet in Pearl Harbour in December 1941, five *Ko-Hyoteki* submarines moved in to help the attack. The result was a failure – all five were lost, and Kazuo Sakamaki was the only survivor of the ten men involved. He became the first Japanese prisoner of war to be captured by the Americans.

A German Neger washed up on an Italian beach in 1944

WASHED UP
Germany had little success with mini-submarines, despite producing about 1,000 of various types, including the *Neger*, *Marder*, *Molch*, and *Biber*. The survival rate of the *Neger*, which was really a torpedo mounted on a torpedo, was never more than 50 per cent.

Periscope

Viewing port

One torpedo on each side

THE BIBER
Fearing that the Allies would invade Europe, the Germans built 324 one-man mini-submarines called *Biber* ("Beaver"). The design was crude, but at least it could dive and surface like a real U-boat. However, the *Biber* proved far too difficult for one person to handle, and many of its pilots died.

US EXPERIMENT
Due to the success of the British X-craft during World War II, postwar midgets continued to be developed. As North America is surrounded by vast stretches of ocean, the US Navy had no need for midgets during the war. However, in 1955, America launched its only experimental midget submarine – *SSX1*.

Miniature periscope

Draught marks – measurements (in feet) of how much of the submarine is underwater

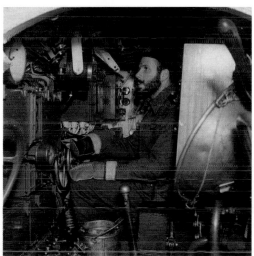

INSIDE A MINIATURE SUB
Conditions in an X-craft were so uncomfortable that during an operation two crews were used. The passage crew consisted of three men, and it was their job to keep the craft in perfect condition while under tow. When the target was about 110 km (68 miles) away, the operational crew of four men took over.

The nuclear age

HARNESSING NUCLEAR ENERGY for propulsion meant that a submarine no longer had to keep coming to the surface to run its engines and charge its battery, since a nuclear reactor does not need oxygen. Nuclear power provided an unlimited source of heat to turn water into steam, so it allowed the submarine to travel huge distances at very high speed – and even enabled it to travel under the North Pole. In addition, it provided all the electrical power needed to refresh the air for the crew. Now a submarine's endurance was limited only by the amount of food it could carry.

THE OLD RESTRICTIONS
Diesel-electric submarines needed regular supplies of fuel, fresh water, and provisions from submarine depot ships. Also, the battery, which powered the boat while submerged, had to be recharged every day, forcing the ship to surface to access air for engine combustion and crew comfort. This put it at high risk of detection and attack.

NUCLEAR LEGACY
The arrival of the nuclear bomb was a shattering event that marked the end of World War II. But even as the bombs exploded over Nagasaki and Hiroshima, scientists were finding new ways to harness this force – including a more efficient means of powering submarines.

"Nautilus under way on nuclear power."

NAUTILUS COMMANDER WILLIAM ANDERSON
17th January 1955

NAUTILUS IN NEW YORK
The world's first nuclear-powered submarine was USS *Nautilus*, launched in 1954. Shown here on a flag-waving visit to New York, *Nautilus* travelled for great distances submerged. But it was her sister submarine, USS *Triton*, that in 1960 was the first to travel 57,947 km (36,014 miles) around the world non-stop under the water, taking just 76 days. The first man to circumnavigate the world, Ferdinand Magellan, took three years to complete the same journey between 1519–22.

Reactor | Heat from reactor boils water into steam. | Steam generator | Steam drives turbine. | Propeller spins.

STEAM SCIENCE
Using heat from the nuclear reaction, water is turned to steam which drives a turbine that spins to turn a shaft with a propeller on the end. As the steam cools, it condenses back into water and the cycle starts again.

UNDER THE ICE
Unhampered by the need to seek fresh air on a daily basis, nuclear submarines could now sail under the Polar ice cap. In 1959, USS *Nautilus* passed under the North Pole. Nine days later, USS *Skate* (above) completed the same route, but surfaced through the thin ice on eight occasions, allowing the sailors to sled on the ice and collect ice water as a souvenir.

NUCLEAR SHIPS
Both the US and the Soviet Union tested their nuclear power systems on ships before fitting them in submarines. The first US nuclear-powered ship was the freighter *Savannah*. The Soviets placed their nuclear power in the *Lenin*, an ice-breaker, which kept open the winter sea lanes to Leningrad (now St Petersburg).

Lenin breaking the ice

SOVIET DEVELOPMENTS
The Soviet Union's first hunter-killer submarine (SSN) came into service in 1958 (pp. 42–43), and the *Leninsky Komsomol*, commemorated on this stamp, sailed under the North Pole in 1962.

INSIDE A NUCLEAR SUBMARINE
The plentiful supply of electricity, fresh water, fresh air, and three hot meals a day made life onboard USS *Nautilus* quite comfortable for the crew. They enjoyed entertainment such as films and music to pass the time between on-duty watches.

Balance of power

Aᴛᴇʀ ᴡᴏʀʟᴅ ᴡᴀʀ ɪɪ, the world was divided into two main power blocks – the West (NATO), led by the democratic United States, and the East (Warsaw Pact) led by the communist Soviet Union. The Warsaw Pact could have overrun NATO with its huge numbers of troops and machines, so the West had to stay ahead in weapons technology. The conflict between the East and the West became known as the Cold War, and the technological battle, the Arms Race. The Cold War was won underwater, as the Soviet Union ran out of money in its bid to match the western submarines. Both fleets are reduced now that the Cold War is over, but they still patrol to deter any would-be nuclear-armed rogue states.

US Seawolf-Class
(9,142 tonnes)

French
Le Redoutable-Class
(9,000 tonnes)

THE NUCLEAR RACE
Admiral Gorshkov, Head of the Soviet Navy, and Admiral Rickover, Head of the US Navy's Nuclear Power Agency, were the "fathers" of the Soviet and US nuclear submarine fleets. They engaged in an almost personal battle of development that led to two massive fleets of missile carriers (SSBNs) and attack submarines (SSNs) costing billions of dollars.

Gorshkov

Rickover

BALANCE OF TERROR
Nuclear submarines carrying nuclear missiles (SSBNs) were the ultimate weapon of the Cold War. They were designed and supported to deliver an overwhelming response against any nuclear weapon aggressor. The western SSBNs were mobile and undetectable, and American missiles like this Polaris A3 were capable of carrying nuclear bombs over thousands of miles.

SPY GAMES
Intelligence of the other side's intentions was an important feature of the Cold War. Both sides used satellites to monitor rival submarine bases from space. Orbital satellites passed over their targets at regular intervals, while geo-stationary satellites kept a target area under constant observation.

Massive missile deck

British
Vanguard-Class
(15,900 tonnes)

Orbital satellite

Russian
Typhoon-Class
(26,500 tonnes)

Russian Oscar-Class
(18,300 tonnes)

Pump-jet propulsion

Missile tubes

US Los Angeles-Class
(6,927 tonnes)

Two Delta hulls joined together

Intercontinental ballistic missile

Access hatch

PROJ
41
40
9
8
7
5

THE SUBMARINE ARMS RACE
Western submarines always held
the tactical advantage because of
their superior listening capability and
noise quietening techniques. Soviet
submarine design therefore focused
on size, speed, and survivability,
which included diving to great
depths. The Russian Typhoon-
Class was, at 26,500 tonnes, the
largest submarine ever built.

US Ohio-Class
(18,750 tonnes)

END GAME
Although Soviet submarine improvements were
closing the gap in the late 1980s, the economic strain
put on the Soviet Union by the Arms Race led to the
Warsaw Bloc's collapse and the fall of the Berlin Wall.
The era of "Mutually Assured Destruction" was over.

Anatomy of a nuclear submarine

Search
and attack
periscopes
covered with
RAM (Radar
Absorbent
Material)

THE SHIFT FROM CONVENTIONAL to nuclear power in submarines was life-changing for their crews. Gone were the single-deck craft that smelt of diesel oil, throbbed with the sound of the engines, and had stale air. In their place came the hum of ventilation fans, multi-deck facilities, and reasonable living space. Unlimited electrical power generated by steam turbines was a luxury that saw the introduction of air purification machinery, plentiful drinking water, and even showers. In the West, boats operated on a single nuclear reactor, while those of the Soviet fleet relied on two. Both East and West developed two types of nuclear submarine – comparatively small and fast hunter-killers (SSNs), and enormous missile carriers (SSBNs).

The size and speed of a
modern nuclear submarine
requires a much taller conning
tower than in the past in order
to remain stable.

BOOMERS
The largest submarines are "Boomers" – the missile carriers that normally go to sea on deterrent patrol for periods of between 60 and 90 days. This British example is a Resolution-Class, introduced in 1967. It carried 16 Polaris missiles as well as six torpedo tubes. Submarines replaced bomber aircraft as the method of delivering nuclear weapons.

Single multi-bladed
propeller

Emergency
propulsion motor

Main engine
coupled to the
propeller's shaft

Steam turbo
generators for
electrical generation

USS SEAWOLF
Originally, 29 boats in the Seawolf-Class – America's newest and fastest attack submarine – were to be built. Due to the cost, this has now been scaled down to just three, and they will be succeeded by the more advanced Virginia-Class. Seawolf was commissioned in 1997, and can carry up to 50 torpedoes and missiles, or 100 mines. The submarine is very quiet and capable of going on multi-missions.

REACTOR ROOM
The heart of the modern submarine, the nuclear reactor is closely monitored at all times. The reactor is normally in the stern half of the submarine, and is started several hours before the boat is scheduled to leave port. If required, it could then remain active for years.

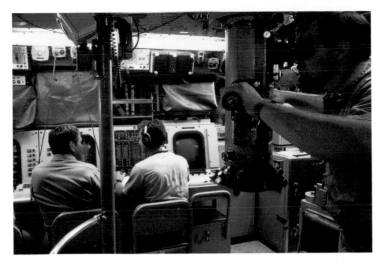

THE ATTACK CENTRE

In the past, the captain of a submarine had only his periscope to use to identify and attack his prey. Today, he has an array of sensors and computers to detect, identify, and work out the attack solution of his target. He may also have a selection of weapons with which to conduct the attack, including the ability to guide his torpedoes directly onto his target.

The inside of a torpedo tube on a Trident submarine

TORPEDOES AWAY!

The days when torpedoes were pulled into position by crews with ropes are over. Now, a 1,360-kg (3,000-lb) American Mk 48 will be moved on skids controlled by hydraulic systems. This is much safer for the crew, and allows weapons officers to make quick changes between the type of weapons loaded in the torpedo tubes.

"Nest" of masts

Thick bulkheads divide main compartments of submarine.

Staircase joins three decks of missile areas.

Forward crew and mess decks

Six torpedo tubes in the bow

Missile inspection hatch

Missile tube

Attack centre

Resolution Class – one of the quietest submarines ever built

Torpedo room

THE DRIVING SEAT

Modern submarines are similar to aircraft, and the crew who "fly" them are called planesmen. Strapped into their seats like airline pilots, their responsibility is to keep the boat straight and level by careful use of the bow and stern hydroplanes. As with a jet fighter, a modern submarine can take on large angles when manoeuvring at speed – hence the restraining straps

Planesmen controlling the angle and depth of a submarine

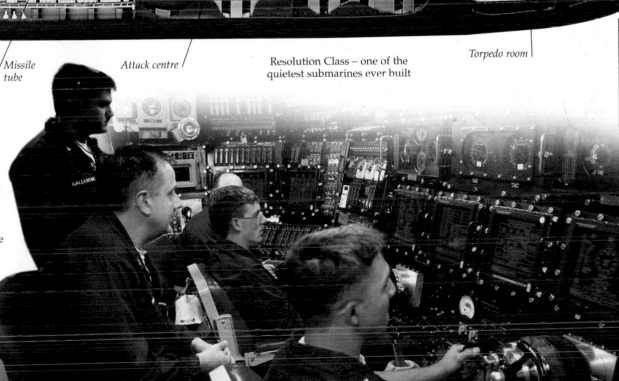

Flying the flag

In 1914, a British submarine commander, Lieutenant Max Horton of HMS *E9*, raised a flag bearing a skull and crossbones when he returned from patrol. He had sunk the German battlecruiser *Hela*, and he flew his home-made ensign in response to an earlier accusation that all submarines were pirates! Horton started a tradition that was adopted by other submarine services, and which continues to this day. During World War II, US submarines, as well as flying their colourful battle flags, would also tie a broomstick to a periscope if they had achieved a "clean sweep" and had sunk all their targets.

MISSION ACCOMPLISHED
The crew of HMS *United* display a record of their latest success on return to port after a wartime cruise. The skull and crossbones became a centrepiece of British flags. The eggtimer was special to *United* because she had suffered a sustained depth charge attack.

Insignia on American Gato-Class USS *Piranha*

German U-boat *U-564*

German U-boat *U-124*

German U-boat *U-124*

PERSONAL INSIGNIA
Submarines always carried individual insignia on their conning towers – usually created by the boat's commander. They became a permanent fixture and would often be handed on when there was a change of command.

Silver Star

Nazi flag represents sinking of German ship.

Congressional Medal of Honour

Naval Crosses

Bronze Star

Red Sun flags for Japanese merchant ships sunk or damaged

Symbol for sinking 7 small ships under 500 tonnes each

Commando raid on railway on land

Symbol for bombardment of a target such as a factory

Rising Sun flags for Japanese warships sunk or damaged

SUCCESS OF THE HUNTER
As her battle ensign signifies, USS *Barb* was one of the most successful of the American Gato-Class submarines. Her flag (above) boasts a total of 57 attacks. In addition, several symbols represent the medals awarded to the submarine. US submarines such as *Barb* decimated the Japanese surface fleet, sinking 60 per cent of its total tonnage. But like all submarine services during both world wars, they paid a heavy price in submariners' lives for their success.

American flag

USS *Ray*

USS *William H. Bates*

USS *Hyman G. Rickover*

NATIONAL EMBLEMS

On entering and leaving harbour, all submarines take the rare opportunity to hoist their national flag above the conning tower. In some cases, a surface cruise will result in a battered flag that then becomes a prized part of the boat's history, as with these flags of the American and British Navies.

British flag

MEMORABILIA

Submarines' individual emblems were also displayed on memorabilia. These cigarette lighters were produced for submarine crews, who became members of old comrade associations after leaving naval service. Even in retirement, submariners remain proud of their achievements.

CREW PATCHES

Pride in your vessel has always played a part in naval life, and these shoulder patches were worn by the entire crew of the respective submarines. In wartime, crews do not carry individual ship identification, as this information could help enemy agents assess overall naval strength at sea.

THE LAUNCH

Celebrations mark the launch of USS *Albany* from the shipyards of Virginia, USA, in 1987. All submarines going down the slip have badges similar to this on their noses. Combining a motto and a picture, the badge is very personal to a submarine. In harbour, submarines put up their badge for decoration until they are about to sail for sea.

Life on board

THE SUBMARINE is a fighting machine, and so the first priority is fitting into the hull all the equipment that allows it to do its job with maximum efficiency. The crew comes second, and they have to squeeze in wherever there is space. In small World War II diesel-driven submarines this meant sleeping with torpedoes, and living cheek by jowl with one's shipmates. Electrical power from the battery was needed for the propulsion motors, so there was little to spare for cooking and making fresh water. Ditching refuse and refreshing the air could only be achieved once a day when the submarine surfaced at night. The result was a noisy, cramped, smelly, and dangerous place to live and work.

A SPELL ON DECK
Lookouts were the eyes and ears of a submarine when surfaced. They enjoyed daylight and fresh air but, like this World War I U-boat crew, had to be ready to act at the first sign of danger.

Most boxes were plain, but some had elaborate decoration.

A portrait of the box's owner

Family pictures

Letter from home

Sewing kit

Medal

KEEPING FIT
Activity helps to keep a crew mentally and physically fit. Japanese submariners are seen here exercising on deck while the boat is in harbour. During wartimes, such exercise would be impossible. A submarine caught on the surface with this many men on deck would have been an easy target.

SHIP'S CATERING
Submariners shared their living space with sacks of potatoes, boxes of vegetables, and loaves of bread. The galley – the kitchen – was tiny, and there was only one hot meal per day, served when the submarine surfaced at night. Tinned food of all sorts – sardines, vegetables, butter and jam – was the staple diet.

DITTY BOX
In the British Royal Navy, the only private space that most submariners enjoyed was a small wooden box, called a "ditty box". Here they would keep letters, photographs, money, luxuries, toiletries, and a "housewife" – their sewing kit for making repairs to their uniforms.

Razor

Cigarette lighter

MASCOTS AND CHARMS

Submariners were superstitious and frequently carried good-luck charms, such as dolls like this. Horseshoes were often hung in the living quarters as they were also thought to bring good luck. The mascots all had the same purpose – to ward off death. The most popular superstition in any submarine was that it was good luck to maintain a routine. Everything was done in the same way and at the same time.

FUN AND GAMES

Crewmen indulged in a variety of games known to children all over the world. The most popular of these was ludo, nicknamed "uckers". This particular game required a combination of luck and skill, but crewmen were so competitive that to be the uckers champion became a major achievement. Cards and dominoes were also popular, but gambling was banned.

SHARED REST

On board, long hours could be spent waiting for action, or simply conserving oxygen if a submarine was forced to remain under the surface. In many cases, two crewmen would alternately share one bed – known as "hot bunking". While one was on duty, the other would rest or sleep until it was his turn to go on watch.

LUXURIES

During World War I and II, almost every adult smoked. Submariners were no exception, despite the constant battle for fresh air. Government cigarettes came with encouraging propaganda messages and were often used to trade for chocolate and other luxuries. Rum was also traded for favours – exchanged for "sippers" and "gulpers" from a crewman's bottle.

Tobacco box

WATER SHORTAGE

This German U-boat crewman is using a makeshift bath filled with seawater. Standard facilities were much more basic than this. During World War II, the general allowance was half an inch of water in a washing bowl. The priority was to brush your teeth, then wash your face and socks.

How things have changed

The introduction of nuclear power meant that submarines could stay at sea for months on end so, although the machine remained the most important consideration on board, care for the crew's morale also became a concern. The multi-decked nuclear-powered craft offers the biggest luxury of all – space. Together with odour-free air, silence, and even limited privacy, conditions have improved dramatically. The ability to stay clean and fresh, eat well, take exercise, and relax in a variety of ways are now routine features of a modern submariner's life.

EXERCISE
The enormous length of a missile submarine provides an unusual opportunity for daily jogging. The captain of the Trident-missile-armed submarine USS *Alabama* is seen here on a run – 12 times around the missile area equals a kilometre. Other facilities often included on submarines today are exercise machines, and one class of Russian submarine even has a swimming pool and a sauna.

SLEEPING QUARTERS
Living space on nuclear submarines varies with the type of boat. The sheer size of missile submarines offers greater crew space, while hunter-killers are much more confined with sailors still sleeping between racks of torpedoes. Crew members on the USS *Alabama*, seen here resting in their bunkbeds, have individual reading lights to offset the muted red lighting. In addition there are fresh air ducts, earphones connected to the on-board entertainment system, and a small curtain for privacy. Even though the passing of day to night goes largely unnoticed, routine is maintained by switching the lights to red to indicate it is night.

WASHING AND SHAVING
Fresh water in a nuclear submarine is produced by boiling sea water in distillers, condensing the steam given off, and storing the water in tanks. The salty residue, known as brine, is then pumped over the side. This process uses a lot of electricity, which is not available from the limited storage battery in conventional submarines. Crews can now wash, shower, and shave regularly, as a submariner is doing here on USS *Jacksonville*. There is even a laundry.

WOMEN ON BOARD

Until recently most submariners have been male, and even today war-time crews are likely to be all-male. Less physically demanding peacetime patrols offer wider scope for women to join underwater crews. Canadian Lieutenant Karen O'Connell became the first female to volunteer for submarine service in 1995 and has been to sea with both the Canadian and Norwegian Navies.

TECHNOLOGY

When off watch, submariners use personal computers for educational purposes and computer games. Other advancements in technology over the years have seen the introduction of videos to replace the traditional film projectors. This allows many more films to be carried on board – submarines often carry about 400 now, which are exchanged for new releases when the vessel reaches port. Despite the arrival of the internet and the mobile phone, submariners and their families must accept that they will be out of contact with each other for months at a time.

Chef on a Russian submarine

THE GALLEY

Unlike ships, submarines enjoy stability under the surface, and the crew suffer less seasickness. As a result, there is demand for a wider selection of meals. The submarine's cook used to be any member of the crew who showed enthusiasm for the kitchen, and he had to operate from a galley no bigger than a broom cupboard. Today, there are four chefs on each vessel, trained to the highest standards, with excellent cooking facilities. There are even ongoing contests between chefs.

THE MESS

Food for the crew is the only limitation on how long a submarine can be submerged in peacetime. Deep freezers, chillers, cool rooms, and ice cream machines ensure a supply of quality food, 24 hours a day. Submarines usually go to sea with 90 days of supplies, although extras are carried to cater for an extended voyage or an emergency situation. The messes remain the social centres of a submarine, and mealtimes offer the opportunity for crew members to get together and exchange all the latest news about their working and personal lives.

Up periscope!

THE PERISCOPE IS LIKE AN eye on top of a pole, which when pushed out of the water enables the captain of a submerged submarine to see what is happening at the surface. Until recently, the periscope was the primary method both of detecting a target and then calculating how best to attack with the torpedoes. Today, a submarine's listening devices, such as sonar, are much more important than its "eyes". But when a modern periscope is exposed above the waves, it is not just looking – it also collects electronic data through an integrated aerial, gets a satellite "fix", and receives communications broadcasts from headquarters on land.

USING THE PERISCOPE
Too much use of the periscope could lead to the target taking evasive action or, worse still, the submarine coming under attack. It took great skill on the part of the submarine captain to show only the tip of the periscope above the surface and absorb all the information about the target (such as range and speed) in less than 15 seconds.

Left grip

High power lens

Low power lens

TARGET DESTROYED
In wartime, a submarine's standard technique for detecting an enemy ship was through binoculars when the submarine was at the surface. The submarine would follow tell-tale wisps of smoke on the horizon, and manoeuvre into an attacking position ahead of the target. It would then dive and use its attack periscope to complete the final stages of the approach, before firing a salvo of torpedoes.

INSIDE A PERISCOPE
This German World War I periscope shows the exterior and interior of a typical U-boat periscope. It provides two different views – low power makes the target 1.5 times larger, while high power makes it 6 times larger.

The periscope fits into this weatherproof brass casing.

IDENTIFYING THE TARGET
It was essential for the submarine to know what it was attacking. Warships could counter-attack and so usually they were avoided, unless they were a prime target such as an aircraft carrier or a battleship. The submarine's crew would refer to *Jane's Fighting Ships*, the standard illustrated guide to warships and their operational capabilities.

Periscope trainer models

PERISCOPE TRAINING
Many navies find model ships help when training sailors in how to use the periscope. As a reminder, the most obvious parts of each ship are made bigger on the models. Submariners quickly work out how to recognize every ship.

SEARCH PERISCOPE

The larger of a submarine's two periscopes is the search periscope, which has two eyepieces for observing the horizon for ships and the sky for patrolling aircraft. In coastal waters, it is used to take navigational observations. The left grip controls the elevation of the search, and the right the magnifying power. The periscope also contains a sextant for star sight navigation, a split-image ranging system, and filters to reduce glare.

The captain works out how far away the target is when two split images meet.

Access for stills camera

Ranging information

Binocular eyepieces

Right grip

Set up information

SPLIT-IMAGE RANGING

A submarine needs three pieces of information to attack a target: its bearing, its range, and its aspect (the angle between the submarine and the target). The first and last clues are obtained through observation. The range is calculated by tilting a half-silvered mirror on the periscope to split the target image as shown.

CAUGHT ON CAMERA

Gathering information from major ports and naval bases is an important task for submarines. Still cameras such as this US Navy camera record the view through the periscope, and are usually attached to it. Video cameras are now incorporated into the system and can relay their signals to viewing screens throughout the submarine.

The ring to join to the periscope

VIEW ABOVE WATER

USS *Alaska*, seen here in Resurrection Bay, Alaska, has two masts raised. The tall one behind is a communications mast, and the shorter one ahead is a periscope. The submarine is moving quite quickly, as can be seen from the feather (wake) being left by the masts as they cut through the water. This is a peacetime scenario. During war, the submarine would not expose so much mast, which could be easily picked up on radar, and it would move slowly to avoid a wake.

Submarine weapons

As a WEAPON OF WAR, the submarine only realized its full potential when it successfully fired a nuclear missile to hit a land target thousands of kilometres away. The submarine was no longer limited to war at sea. While maintaining its original role as a torpedo-equipped ship hunter and intelligence gatherer, the submarine has expanded its weaponry to include missiles and torpedoes with broader ranges. In the 1990s, the Cold War ended and fleet sizes were reduced. Many American submarines removed their ballistic missiles as the need for deterrent weapons was reduced. Tomahawk cruise missiles replaced them, as tactical capability gained importance.

TARGET CALCULATION

In the early days of submarine warfare, the captain would have to calculate the speed and distance of the target, its size and depth, and the speed at which the torpedo would travel. Calculating the correct time to fire was difficult because the submarine and target were always moving. This World War II German calculator improved accuracy, although the basic tactic was to fire a "spread" of up to six torpedoes to cover inaccuracies in estimations.

Torpedoes in the bow

THE TORPEDO ROOM

Small torpedo rooms have given way to huge compartments packed with a variety of weapons. Torpedo tubes were traditionally placed in the bow and stern sections of a submarine. However, many modern submarines have moved the bow tubes and replaced them with modern sonar displays to locate and "hear" their target.

Loading Mk 48 torpedo on USS *Haddock*

This gyroscope was fitted to German torpedoes in World War II.

TORPEDO ON TRACK

The gyroscope keeps the torpedo travelling in a straight line towards its target. It was first introduced in 1895 by the British engineer Robert Whitehead, the inventor of the torpedo. Since then, there have been major changes to the design. Sound-seeking torpedoes now hunt their prey, while wire-guided torpedoes can be steered with great accuracy, even passing information back to their controller.

LOADING RULES

Loading weapons onto a submarine requires accuracy. Torpedoes are inserted at a 45° angle to the hull. Intercontinental missiles, such as Trident, leave the Earth's atmosphere and plunge back onto their target, so they must be lowered vertically into launch tubes.

MISSILE HATCHES
The greater size of the modern submarine has enabled silos of missiles to be mounted outside the hull in vertical tubes. Shown here is a nest of Tomahawk Land Attack missiles in a US Navy Los Angeles-Class SSN. The missiles are blasted from tubes by compressed air, and their rocket motors fire once the sea's surface is cleared. The hatch is then closed and the silo drained of water.

BALLISTIC MISSILES
Ballistic missiles carry nuclear warheads, and Polaris was the first submarine-launched missile of this kind. Tested in 1960, it sent a warhead 4,000 km (2,485 miles). By the 1980s, Trident replaced it with a range of 8,047 km (5,000 miles), a three-stage rocket motor, and 14 nuclear weapons in the warhead.

MINES
One of the greatest menaces to the submarine is the sea mine, lurking at a wide range of depths, ready to explode and cause huge damage. During the first Gulf War (1990–91), the US Navy lacked anti-mine facilities and this led to extensive damage to support ship USS *Tripoli* when it struck an Iraqi mine.

CRUISE MISSILE
The Tomahawk Land Attack cruise missile (TLAM) is a low-flying weapon capable of remaining below radar barriers at high subsonic speeds. Launched from vertical tubes inside attack submarines, the missile uses satellite information to ensure it arrives on target at the exact time required.

SEA SKIMMER
Fitted to all US Navy and Royal Navy attack submarines, the Sub-harpoon can be fired from surface ships and aircraft, too. Armed with a 203-kg (448-lb) high-explosive warhead, it is a radar-controlled sea skimmer with a range of 97 km (60 miles).

Sub-harpoon missile

HMS *Sybil* in World War II

GUNS ON SUBMARINE DECK
In both world wars, submarines tried to conserve their limited number of torpedoes. The alternative was to surface and use deck guns to destroy their targets instead. The gun became an inappropriate weapon as torpedo ranges and accuracy improved. Since then, it has been totally phased out.

"Polaris is... to be instantly ready in peacetime to launch missiles in retaliation for a nuclear attack, with the aim of preventing, by its presence and readiness, such a catastrophe from ever occurring. If Polaris ever has to be used, therefore, it has failed."

VICE ADMIRAL SIR ARTHUR HEZLET

Anti-submarine warfare

AIRBORNE THREAT
In World War II, submarines spent most of their time on the surface, so aircraft were the best way to spot and bomb them. The American-built long-range B24 Liberator was a success, closing the "Atlantic gap" created by the limited flying range of previous aircraft. Aircraft were credited with sinking 288 U-boats.

DEPTH CHARGING
Traditionally, the most effective way to sink a submarine was to use depth charges. These were rolled off the stern of a surface ship. The canister of high explosive inside the charge was set in advance to explode at the estimated depth of the submarine below.

DURING WORLD WAR I, the only way to detect a submarine was with the human eye. Then, the only option was to try ramming it. The depth charge arrived in 1915 and transformed the way a submarine could be attacked. By World War II, electronic "eyes" were invented – sonar sound-seekers beneath the waves, and radar above. These were joined by another powerful weapon in 1944 – the anti-submarine homing torpedo. These detection devices and weapons were fitted firstly into warship escorts, and then into aircraft, which were flown either from shore or from aircraft carriers. The helicopter has recently joined the battle, and to complete the anti-submarine team is the most lethal anti-submarine weapon of all – another submarine.

Anti-torpedo nets

PROTECTION
Once the threat of the submarine was noted, navies started devising methods of protection. The first of these were nets, placed across narrow channels and around warships. These were backed up by anti-submarine minefields.

Depth charge on its way to a submarine target

SUCCESS RATE
Depth charges destroyed only nine U-boats between 1915 and 1917. As a result, these weapons were further developed and in 1918, 22 U-boats were sunk. Almost 600 of the 785 U-boats lost during World War II fell to charges. At first they were dropped from the hunting ship, but later they were fired from a distance, giving the submarine little chance of escape.

MODERN ANTI-SUB WARFARE

Nuclear submarines have the ability to hear, seek, and destroy underwater attackers. This means they are now as important as surface ships for protecting large fleets such as aircraft carrier groups. These modern submarines can easily match, and often beat, the speed and range of surface craft. Together with assistance from aircraft, the submarine has never been more watched from the skies, from the surface, or from underwater.

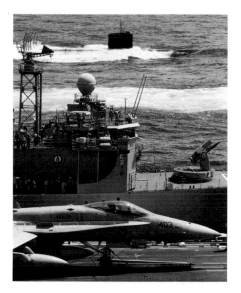

Submarine protecting fleet

Extra long-range fuel tanks

Surface search radar

MAD boom at the stern

Searchlight for target identification

WATCHERS ABOVE

Aircraft such as the RAF Nimrod were specially built to find submarines in the waters below. In the tail of this aircraft is the Magnetic Anomaly Detector (MAD) apparatus, which can detect a large moving metal object underwater.

HELICOPTER HUNTERS

Most modern frigates and destroyers carry an ASW helicopter. The ability of the helicopter to find and destroy submarines has improved in recent years. It can hop from point to point over the ocean at random, and it is equipped with both active and passive listening devices. It will also carry at least two homing torpedoes for attack.

Seahawk ASW helicopter

Radar dome for surface search

Frigates carry guns, missiles, and helicopters.

ANTI-SUBMARINE FRIGATES

Powered by jet engines originally intended for civil and military aircraft, these high-speed ships are capable of covering a lot of ground looking for submarines. As well as searching, their other strength is to attack submarines from further away by launching their helicopter to where they think the submarine is hiding.

Anti-submarine torpedo

Helicopter drops device into water to listen for submarines.

SILENCE IS GOLDEN

Location by sound is now the biggest threat, with aircraft, ships, and hunter-killer submarines listening for their prey. Microphones are even placed on the sea bed of known submarine routes to detect any sounds.

ANTI-SUB SUB

An anti-sub submarine is the most lethal weapon because it is can go to the same depths as the hunted submarine and seek out its hiding places. Western anti-sub submarines were quieter and had superior listening devices to their Soviet counterparts until late into the Cold War. Anti-sub submarines such as the Russian Akula-Class (right) arrived to close the capability gap. The Akula-Class was quieter, more streamlined, and a very efficient searcher. As Akula-Class submarines were large, they carried lots of listening devices.

Underwater listening device

Communication and navigation

F OR A SUBMARINER, the world is three-dimensional – everything is either above the surface (satellites and aircraft), on the surface (ships and land), or below the surface (changes in temperature and sea-bed trenches). To consider and deal with all of these things, a submarine relies almost entirely on radio waves. But the submarine only listens – transmitting is risky and rare. Information is constantly coming in on screens and charts, sent from satellites and other communications systems. The heart of navigation on a submarine is the Ships Inertial Navigation System (SINS). Used since the 1950s, these sensors adjust to movement, with SINS readouts all over the submarine.

Search periscope

Surface warning light

Commun -ications mast

CARRIER PIGEON
Before radio waves transformed communication, the only option for submarines to communicate when out of sight of land was to use carrier pigeons. Pigeons with messages strapped to their legs were launched off the side of the vessel to headquarters.

A German operator decoding from the Enigma machine

ANTENNAE FOREST
Although extending a periscope is one of the most dangerous moves a submarine can make, the equipment for radio and visual sightings must still be available at the top of the conning tower. For the submarine to grab a message ("dump") from a satellite, the communications masts must be raised out of the conning tower, as seen here on this Seawolf submarine.

SECRET CODES
Communicating radio wave messages in secret is essential during wartime. During World War II, the Germans developed the complex Enigma machine that transmitted messages in code. When the Allies captured this decoding machine from a sinking German U-boat, they cracked the code, read the radio traffic, and this helped to win the war at sea.

Antenna to avoid detection

TRAILING ANTENNA
A trailing antenna is used when a submarine wants to listen to routine communications without coming to periscope depth. The Very Low Frequency (VLF) signals take a long time to receive, but there is no risk of detection. The submarine moves slowly, listening to news from home, tactical signals, and intelligence received from shore.

THE SATELLITE

Communications satellites are like big telephone exchanges in the sky. A sub identifies itself with a number to receive messages, which have been fed to the satellite by global headquarters. Subs can only transmit and receive information at Super High Frequency (SHF) via a satellite. An attack submarine raises its mast to collect information when it needs to.

Solar panels create satellite transmission power.

Satellite aerials or transponders

ECHOSOUNDER

An echosounder is used to find out how far away the sea bed is from the submarine. By squirting a short pulse of energy that hits the sea bed, an echo is created. The echosounder hears this echo – the distance can be calculated by however long it takes to come back. This is even more useful under ice when submariners set their echosounders to bounce a signal off both the sea bed and the ice. These two signals ensure that the submarine moves safely between the two.

Echosounder transmitter and receiver

SEXTANT

Navigation by the sun, moon, and stars has been practised for thousands of years. Before the introduction of electronic navigation aids and when out of sight of land, the geographical position of a submarine was worked out with a sextant. This tool measured the angle of the sun, moon, and stars against the horizon and converted the results into bearing lines. The sextant is still carried on submarines today.

PLOTTING ON MAP

Even the most advanced submarine must use charts to navigate in and out of harbours. Using dividers and a parallel slide on a map, the navigating officer calculates where the submarine is and checks there are no dangers along the way. Depth of water, wrecks, and rocks are vital information as the officer plots the course. Electronic charts exist today, although a paper chart is carried, too.

The pulse of energy is released here.

Various colours represent the different depths of the contours.

Contour image of a continental shelf on the sea bed

Contour image of the ocean floor off California, USA

BOTTOM CONTOUR NAVIGATION

If a submarine does not want to raise a mast for a satellite "fix", Bottom Contour Navigation is the slower alternative. This is navigation from known contours of the ocean floor. The echosounder helps to draw the shape of what is below the submarine, and parts of the ocean are mapped in such detail that the resulting fix is extremely accurate.

Submarine disasters

The doomed *Maria*

THE FIRST DISASTER
In June 1774, Englishman John Day took a dive in the boat *Maria* and became the first ever casualty of a submarine disaster. Before he went down, he told people he would go to the bottom of Plymouth Harbour and stay there for 12 hours. Unfortunately, he wrongly calculated the weight of the ballast needed to dive. Neither he nor *Maria* were ever seen again.

SUBMARINES ARE DANGEROUS PLACES to work in. Not only must they resist the ocean, which is squeezing them under great pressure and could quickly sink them in a flood, they also carry high explosive weapons, oil and air supplies, high voltage electrical systems, and – in many cases – a nuclear reactor that must be carefully maintained. These dangers are overcome by the skill of their builders, who use the highest quality materials, and the operation of the crew, who are highly trained to react instantly to a disaster. But accidents do happen.

Lieutenant Sakuma in full naval uniform

PERSONAL APOLOGY
In April 1910, a Japanese Navy submarine was diving, but it did not shut a valve quickly enough to keep the water out. The boat flooded and sank. Unable to surface, and running out of oxygen, the boat's captain, Lieutenant Sakuma wrote a personal letter of apology to his Emperor just before he and his crew of 14 died. He finished by asking simply "please look after our families."

Sakuma's letter was found by a salvage team.

The conning tower survived the explosion.

The bow was cut away by the salvage team.

K-Class submarines accompanying surface fleet

THE BATTLE OF MAY ISLAND
The steam-powered K-Class was the clumsiest design ever produced by the British Navy. Its failure was legendary, most notably in a major exercise in 1918 that became known as the Battle of May Island. By the end of the day, two K-Class submarines had been sunk and several damaged in separate incidents involving collisions. Many British submariners lost their lives.

THE *KURSK* DISASTER
The accident that sank the massive Russian nuclear submarine *Kursk* in August, 2000, was caused first by a torpedo explosion, and was then made much worse by a subsequent fire that caused more explosions. All 118 crewmen died. The shattered hull of *Kursk* was located and raised by a Norwegian salvage team. They returned the wreck to its Arctic base.

Severe damage to the upper deck

The attempt to rescue Thetis

RAISING THE *THETIS*
The greatest peacetime disaster in Royal Navy history was the loss of HMS *Thetis* through flooding during trials off Liverpool in 1939. A massive effort by the crew to save the submarine resulted in the stern coming completely out of the water. When the oxygen ran out, 99 men died, but four escaped. Salvaged and renamed *Thunderbolt*, she was lost in action off Italy in 1943.

SIDON CATASTROPHE
An explosion killed 13 crewmen on the submarine HMS *Sidon* as torpedoes were being loaded on 16 June, 1955. Some of the crew were on the bridge at the time so they escaped unhurt. The accident was caused by high-test peroxide (HTP) – a volatile torpedo fuel. After this disaster, the British Navy stopped using the fuel in its weapons.

Raising the wreck of Sidon

Kursk was placed in a dry dock for examination.

A QUESTION OF SALVAGE
Whenever possible, naval authorities try to raise a sunken submarine in order to work out what caused the disaster. Here, USS *Squalus* is salvaged after sinking in May 1939 with the loss of 26 lives. Despite its association with disaster, *Squalus* was raised and refitted to use throughout World War II.

RESCUE FROM THE DEEP
Two world wars have proved that few crew members survive when a submarine sinks. Peacetime provides a greater chance of helping a boat in trouble. The US, Swedish, and British navies have all built Deep Sea Rescue Vehicles (DSRV), which can assist with getting the crew out of a submarine that has sunk, even at very great depths.

The USN DSRV Mystic being carried by a "mother" submarine

Sub safety

Even a small accident at sea in a submarine can turn into a disaster unless it is dealt with immediately and effectively. A flood or fire pose the greatest threat to survival, and so submariners are trained to spot the smallest leak of water and smell the slightest whiff of smoke. Safety devices such as fire extinguishers are scattered throughout the submarine, and if a small fire threatens to spread, then the crew is capable of mustering a full fire brigade between them. Small leaks are prevented from getting bigger by using valves to isolate the risk. Nevertheless these efforts can fail, and research continues into ways to help crew members escape from subs in danger.

DANGEROUS GASES
Early submarines carried miners' lamps and white mice. These mice would give early warning of a build-up of poisonous gases from engine and battery fumes. Mice squeak when they smell carbon monoxide.

Mice are sensitive to gas leaks and fall ill quickly.

AIR RECYCLING
In a flood, the trapped crew need to breathe while they are attempting to escape and during the ascent to the surface. In 1929, Dr. Robert Davis adapted a breathing apparatus he had developed for coal mine disasters into one that could be used in submarine escape. It was small and compact, like an external lung, and was fitted with an oxygen bottle. Named the Davis Submarine Escape Apparatus (DSEA), it was in service in British Royal Navy submarines until the 1950s.

Hall-Rees escape suits

EARLY ESCAPE SYSTEMS
The first ever submarine escape suit was the Hall-Rees equipment designed in 1907. It was a major step forward because it recognized that a special apparatus was required to allow men to escape from a sunken submarine. However, it was so bulky that it was impractical for the tiny submarines in service at the time.

COPING WITH RADIATION
The areas on board a submarine that contain nuclear material – the reactor compartment and the missile tubes – are built to the highest standards, remotely monitored, and designed to contain any initial mishap. If entry is required into those areas for investigative purposes, then special equipment is worn.

Radiation suit

The DSEA

THREAT FROM FIRE

A fire on board is probably the biggest danger to a modern submarine. Fire spreads quickly in such a cramped area and it is very difficult for submariners to escape a burning vessel that is a long way underwater. Although all submarines today carry breathing apparatus such as this oxygen mask, a fire on the Russian submarine *Komsoletts* in 1989 spread so badly out of control that it melted the hull and sank the submarine, drowning 42 of the crew.

Goggles

Nose-clip

Breathing hood

Oxygen mask to protect the wearer from poisonous gases

Crewmen during a fire drill on the USS *Alabama*

FIRE DRILL

A well-trained submarine crew carry out fire drills and equipment checks at least once a week. Each crew member learns how to wear an emergency breathing mask, and each has an agreed fire position. Some would be trained to wear flame-resistant "fearnought" suits to enable them to tackle the cause of the fire.

Gloves to keep hands warm

Life jacket inflation bottle

Reflective patch to alert attention

ESCAPE SUIT

When HMS *Truculent* collided with a merchant ship on the River Thames in 1952 and was sunk, many of her crew managed to escape from the submarine. To everyone's horror when the story unfolded, it was found that many of those who escaped had died through drowning and extreme cold once they had reached the surface. As a result, the escape suit was introduced. Not only does this provide protection against the cold, but it also protects the skin from fire and allows the survivor to float to the surface where they can be picked up by a rescue team.

ABANDON SHIP

This German-built submarine includes a separate escape section in which the crewmen can group together in an emergency. The section acts like an underwater lifeboat. It is detached from the hull and floated to the surface, where the crew can be rescued.

Double-skinned feet to keep out the cold

Pioneering the depths

DESPITE ENORMOUS PROGRESS OVER the years, manned submarines can still reach only the upper regions of the ocean depths. To go deeper and cope with huge water pressures required the development of two vehicles. The first was the bathysphere – a large steel ball suspended on the end of a cable that could be lifted from a ship and lowered into the water. The second was the bathyscaphe – similar to the submarine, but with a massive flotation compartment and an observation ball underneath. With the arrival of the bathyscaphe, pioneers were finally able to reach the deepest point in the world.

THE FIRST DEEP–SEA EXPLORERS
In the 1920s, William Beebe and Otis Barton both explored their interest in nature. Together, the Americans invented this steel bathysphere, which was lowered into the water with a cable. The first time that Beebe and Barton descended in their bathysphere off Bermuda in 1930, it leaked! With improvements, the bathysphere worked and went deeper than any other design at that time.

UNDERWATER WORLD
By 1934, Beebe and Barton's steel bathysphere had set a world record when it reached depths of 920 m (3,028 ft), taking 11 minutes to reach the end of the cable. Descending beneath the ocean surface, the two explored the sea bed and discovered deep-sea creatures that no one had seen before.

"Man lived with the stars, but the deep sea was beyond his ken."

AUGUSTE PICCARD

Main tank containing 9,047 litres (34,000 gallons) of petrol

ULTIMATE DIVE
On 23 January 1960, Jacques Piccard climbed inside his father Auguste's bathyscaphe, *Trieste*, alongside Donald Walsh, and together they began the journey to the deepest point of the ocean – the Marianas Trench in the Pacific. Five hours later *Trieste* touched bottom at 11,500 m (37,730 ft). Built to resist pressures of up to 200,000 tonnes, the bathyscaphe was, and still is, the only craft to visit the deepest point on Earth.

MASTER OF HEIGHT AND DEPTH
Swiss-born Auguste Piccard took his hot-air balloon 15 km (10 miles) in the sky in 1931 after realizing that gas in the inflated bag would expand as he went higher. In 1948, he turned this theory around by replacing gas with petrol in his bathyscaphe *Trieste*. Iron ballast took Trieste to the bottom of the ocean floor and, once there, special low-density petrol sent the craft back to the surface.

Cousteau's diving saucer, which made 123 dives

Hole for observation

Carbon dioxide removers

Oxygen bottles

Port holes for observation

OBSERVATION CHAMBER
Later deep-sea craft became more advanced, as this example from 1930 shows. Still tethered to the surface, this one man submersible observation chamber was designed to search shipwrecks before divers went down to take a look. The pilot inside would breathe air at normal pressure, and this was then recycled to remove carbon dioxide from the system

DIVING SAUCER
Although Beebe and Piccard broke records, it was Frenchman Jacques Cousteau who opened up the sea to the world. He designed and built diving saucers, like this 1959 model, that could power themselves along the sea floor. Eventually, he created underwater work stations where divers stayed for weeks.

TRIESTE

Ballast tank

Two-man observation sphere

Into the abyss

SINCE WILLIAM BEEBE AND AUGUSTE Piccard laid the foundations for deep-sea exploration in unconventional vessels, a whole new range of submersibles has arrived. Deep Research Vehicles (DRVs) and Remotely Operated Vehicles (ROVs) go much deeper than any modern submarine. Largely unmanned, and produced in their hundreds, these exciting vehicles can also work in conditions beyond the capabilities of ordinary submarines. Many can be controlled by operators on the surface using closed-circuit television. Some can even be switched off and left on the sea floor between projects. These vehicles are exploring our seas as never before.

SUPPORT VESSELS
Although submersibles go to great depths, they are not designed for long-range travel on the surface. This is why modified support ships carry them to working locations. For unmanned submersibles, the support ship is also the base where the underwater controls are operated.

ROBOT HELPERS
ROVs such as robot helper *Argo* (above) assist with underwater missions. Built in 1982 for the US Navy, *Argo* is equipped with five video cameras, two sonar systems, and can be computer-controlled to "fly" at specified depths. Photographer Emory Kristof created the first designs for improving ROVs by adding electronic camera equipment. *Argo* was then updated and became the first to photograph the wreck of *Titanic* in 1985.

Support ship *Nadir* about to launch manned *Nautile* to visit the wreck of *Titanic*

Holland I submarine
33 m (108 ft)

Scuba diver
145 m (476 ft)

SSN nuclear submarine
300 m (984 ft)

Armoured diving suit
600 m (1,968 ft)

URN Deep Submergence rescue vehicle
750 m (2,460 ft)

Alfa deepest submarine
900 m (2,953 ft)

Beebe's bathysphere
1,000 m (3,280 ft)

Sperm whale
1,200 m (3,937 ft)

ABYSSAL ZONE —————————————— **HADAL ZONE** ———————————————————

6,000 m (19,685 ft)

Sea bed

Alvin
4,267 m (13,999 ft)

Nautile
6,000 m (19,685 ft)

MIR
6,000 m (19,685 ft)

Shinkai submersible
6,500 m (21,326 ft)

Deepest fish
8,500 m (27,887 ft)

Trieste
11,500 m (37,730 ft)

SUPER SUBMERSIBLE

The rock star of the submersible world is *Alvin*. This $1,000,000 craft entered service in 1964 and has completed over 3,000 dives. *Alvin*'s underwater visits include locating an American H-bomb on the floor of the Mediterranean, discovering giant tubeworms in the Pacific Ocean, and visiting the wreck of *Titanic*. Once it was even attacked by a swordfish – trapped between *Alvin*'s glass layers, the fish was taken to the surface and cooked for dinner!

Alvin exploring the sea floor

SECRET SUBMERSIBLE

The US Navy's nuclear-powered *NR-1* was top secret for many years, silently performing dozens of deep-sea missions. Still in use today, she was adapted to find lost wreckage and rarely resurfaces during an operation. When the space shuttle *Challenger* crashed in 1986, *NR-1* found the scattered remains. Here, *NR-1* extends its "claw" to lift the wreck of a crashed navy jet.

DEEPEST OF ALL

Most commercial submersibles are built to withstand pressures of up to 300 m (10,000 ft) below the surface. Only a few can go below this depth. However, *Shinkai 6500* is a Japanese manned research submersible that can dive to 6,500 m (21,326 ft), as its name suggests. Completed in 1990, *Shinkai 6500* plays an important part in deep-sea research and predicting earthquakes.

Shinkai 6500

Shipwreck

UNTIL THE ARRIVAL OF deep-sea exploration vehicles, the majority of shipwrecks remained unseen and untouched, except for the occasional shallow water discovery. Now that it is possible to identify and visit the wrecks of maritime disasters, ships such as *Titanic*, *Bismarck*, and *Hood* have become key sites of exploration for historians. Wreck visits will increase at all depths as the fascination surrounding these disasters continues. But historians bringing artefacts to the surface are often accused of "treasure hunting" and "tomb raiding". People question whether it is right to disturb the resting place of so many sailors and passengers.

DEEPEST DEPTHS
Early theory maintained that ships did not fall to the bottom of the oceans, but remained suspended in a mid-pressure area. Underwater exploration revealed this was a myth as wrecks were discovered in the depths. Wrecks lying many miles down in the deepest seas have so far eluded all efforts to find them. The condition of shipwrecks at these depths will be a source of interest to historians.

WRECK LOCATOR
In 1773, the huge British ship *The Royal Captain* carrying 100,000 pieces of valuable Chinese porcelain sank in the South China Sea. It took two centuries and a manned submersible to locate the wreck and recover part of the cargo. Frenchman Franck Goddio calculated the possible location of the disaster before making his discovery. He is seen here with a pilot labelling the rotting timbers of *The Royal Captain* with special foam number tags designed to resist water pressure and stay in position. The submersible is bubble-shaped to view the outstanding features of a shipwreck.

EXPLORER OF THE DEEP
Perhaps the greatest living underwater historian is American Robert Ballard, seen here with a model of *Bismarck*. Using remotely controlled vehicles, he has located and explored a number of famous wrecks, including *Titanic*.

Controllers using robotic arms to mark out the remains of the shipwreck.

296

M95

BROUGHT TO THE SURFACE

Launched in 1985, the French-built *Nautile* is a manned exploration submersible. It is famous for a dive in 1989 during which geologists in the vehicle collected samples that revealed how forces shaped the Earth's crust. The submersible has also investigated wrecks, including *Titanic*.

ON THE SURFACE

While wreck investigation is regarded as historical research, taking artefacts from sunken ships is controversial. *Titanic* hit an iceberg and sank on her maiden voyage in 1912, killing more than 1,500 people. By 1987, *Nautile* had made 32 dives to the ruins of *Titanic*, taking a variety of objects.

Titanic's cherub from the Grand Staircase

The remains of a letter that sank with *Titanic*

Playing cards from *Titanic*

Plaque lies on wreck of *Bismarck*

Bismarck war plaque

Japanese mini-sub

WATERY GRAVE

In 1941, the British and German navies clashed in the Atlantic. Battle Cruiser *Hood* blew up and sank, followed by *Bismarck* – on her first operational cruise. Warships such as these usually carry the protection of being classed as war graves, which cannot be visited. Robert Ballard found both ships and placed commemorative war plaques on the wreckage.

SUB FINDS SUB

The surprise attack by the Japanese Air Force on Pearl Harbour, Hawaii, on 7 December, 1941, is well documented. Less well known is that several Japanese midget submarines provided information in advance for the aircraft – five midgets were sunk in the process. This Type A Japanese midget was discovered in 2002 by the manned Hawaii Undersea Research Laboratory.

Creatures of the deep

Sɪɴᴄᴇ ᴛʜᴇ 1950s, the rapid development of research submersibles has led to the discovery of an astonishing variety of deep-sea marine life. Expeditions have found all kinds of animals able to live in conditions where humans could not possibly survive. In this mysterious world of almost total darkness, extreme cold, and tremendous pressure, fish and other animals need special adaptations to survive. Food is scarce, and so are breeding partners. Many deep-sea fish are able to generate their own light to lure prey and to attract partners. Every year, new species of fish are identified at massive depths, but this is only a drop in the ocean compared to what is left to explore.

MARINE EXPLORER
French oceanographer Jacques Cousteau (1910–97) is best known for his undersea exploration. His encounters with deep-sea marine life featured in a long-running TV series. Dedicated to protecting the oceans, Cousteau drew worldwide attention to the dangers of oil spills, overfishing, pollution, and waste dumping.

SPECIMEN COLLECTION
In the 1870s, the ship HMS *Challenger* dredged the oceans to collect 13,000 plants and animals, such as this lobster. Today, marine submersibles can collect even delicate creatures in special containers built to withstand the immense pressures at great depths.

Dana viperfish

THE DEEP-SEA ZOO
Living at depths of 900 m (2,955 ft) or more, these fish have many adaptations to the deep-sea environment. Their huge eyes can detect the faintest glimmer of light. Their soft, flexible skeletons are not crushed by the pressure of all the water pressing down on them from above. These fish also have gaping jaws, sharp teeth, and stretchy stomachs that enable them to take full advantage of any food they are lucky enough to find.

Fish develops inside egg sac.

Fangtooth

Rear-facing teeth trap victims inside the mouth.

Young deep-sea anglerfish

Hatchet fish

Viperfish

SPHERE OF OPERATION

The *Johnson Sea-Link* submersible benefits from a huge sphere that gives the two operators a panoramic view of their area of underwater exploration. It is also equipped with external cameras that send pictures to a video monitor inside the craft. The *Sea-Link* was designed to study sea life, and it has a robotic claw and scoop for collecting live specimens such as fish and invertebrates. Fragile creatures are sucked up using a flexible suction hose.

Dragonfish

Dome-like control centre provides maximum vision.

Claw-like arm for collecting marine animals

Light-producing organ flashes on and off to lure prey within range of the dragonfish's jaws.

Banks of light to illuminate the work area

Deep-sea anglerfish

Deep-sea cat shark

The smoker releases a stream of sulphur, which colours the water black.

Huge jaws enable the gulper eel to swallow prey larger than itself.

Gulper eel

BLACK SMOKERS

In parts of the Pacific and Atlantic, superheated water gushes up from cracks in the sea bed. These deep-sea springs, or hydrothermal vents, may be up to 2,500 m (8,200 ft) below the surface. It is usually very cold at such great depths, but water around the vents reaches temperatures of more than 300°C (572°F). The rushing hot water deposits minerals to form "chimneys" called black smokers.

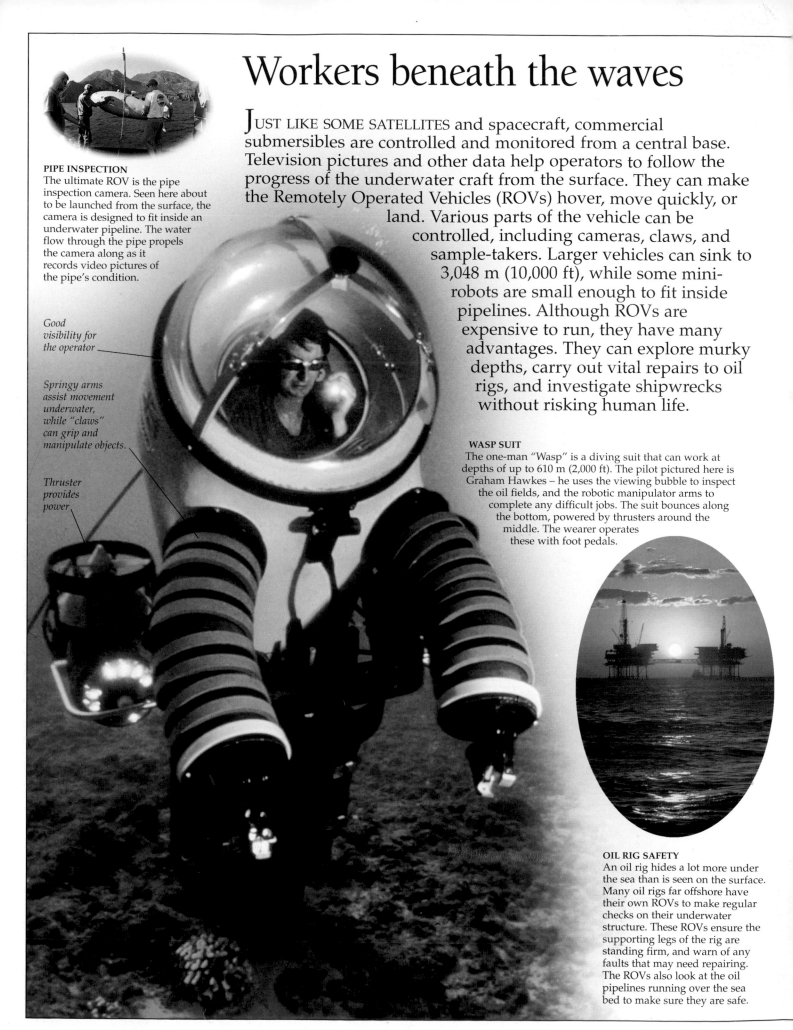

Workers beneath the waves

Just like some satellites and spacecraft, commercial submersibles are controlled and monitored from a central base. Television pictures and other data help operators to follow the progress of the underwater craft from the surface. They can make the Remotely Operated Vehicles (ROVs) hover, move quickly, or land. Various parts of the vehicle can be controlled, including cameras, claws, and sample-takers. Larger vehicles can sink to 3,048 m (10,000 ft), while some mini-robots are small enough to fit inside pipelines. Although ROVs are expensive to run, they have many advantages. They can explore murky depths, carry out vital repairs to oil rigs, and investigate shipwrecks without risking human life.

PIPE INSPECTION
The ultimate ROV is the pipe inspection camera. Seen here about to be launched from the surface, the camera is designed to fit inside an underwater pipeline. The water flow through the pipe propels the camera along as it records video pictures of the pipe's condition.

Good visibility for the operator

Springy arms assist movement underwater, while "claws" can grip and manipulate objects.

Thruster provides power

WASP SUIT
The one-man "Wasp" is a diving suit that can work at depths of up to 610 m (2,000 ft). The pilot pictured here is Graham Hawkes – he uses the viewing bubble to inspect the oil fields, and the robotic manipulator arms to complete any difficult jobs. The suit bounces along the bottom, powered by thrusters around the middle. The wearer operates these with foot pedals.

OIL RIG SAFETY
An oil rig hides a lot more under the sea than is seen on the surface. Many oil rigs far offshore have their own ROVs to make regular checks on their underwater structure. These ROVs ensure the supporting legs of the rig are standing firm, and warn of any faults that may need repairing. The ROVs also look at the oil pipelines running over the sea bed to make sure they are safe.

READY TO EXPLORE
ROVs can view and explore the remains of shipwrecks, as well as possible undersea building sites. This ROV is being lowered into the ocean to examine wrecks off the coast of Cuba. It can also examine the sea floor where a bridge or harbour is about to be built. If the ROV finds a problem, the plans can be changed.

Television pictures from an ROV

Coordinator directs the ROV operators.

UNDERWATER SURVEILLANCE
One of the smallest ROVs in the world, VideoRay is used to investigate tiny spaces and polluted waters that could be dangerous for divers to visit. The controls are similar to those on a video game console and it can go to depths of 150 m (500 ft).

THE CONTROL ROOM
ROVs do many jobs that divers used to do, often at great risk. Thanks to technology, ROV operators can now complete these tasks from the safety of a control room in a ship. The ROV sends back information from the water via a cord, and the operator directs the movements of the craft.

Colour video camera

Electrical control leads

Halogen lights

03-AUG-02
14:25:17
D:161.3FT

ACCIDENT INVESTIGATION
Millions of objects have landed in the sea over the years, and many were the result of accidents. ROVs can help to discover crash sites and investigate the wreckage. In this case, VideoRay was sent down to find the wreck of a car that crashed in 1927. This was one image sent back by VideoRay.

Skis to skid along the sea bed

Manipulator to take items from the search area

Gator trench digger

Giant caterpillar tracks

CABLE LAYERS
The vast ocean floor is crisscrossed by many communication cables. These need to be protected from damage, particularly in the shallow sand of coastlines. Special ROV trench diggers have been developed that drive alongside the cable-laying ship and place the cables inside the trenches.

Subs for fun

Submarine film posters

DESPITE THEIR INVOLVEMENT IN war, submarines became a form of entertainment in the second half of the 20th century. The public was fascinated with these exciting machines, and businesses realized that they could make money out of fun submarines. Lake's idea of a submarine on wheels (p. 20) finally became a reality in Disneyland, USA, where model submarines running on rails took holidaymakers around the park. In the 1960s, world-famous band *The Beatles* made a cartoon film about a yellow submarine. Submarines began to carry tourists, and luxury submarines were built. Now there are even submarine museums and underwater hotels.

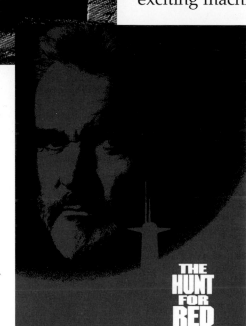

SUBMARINE MOVIES
Submarine films came to life after World War II when they had much more history to base the action on. In particular, German-produced *Das Boot* (1981) showed the reality of being on a U-boat. Later, *The Hunt for Red October* (1990) provided a look at a nuclear submarine involved in war. Famous fictional characters such as James Bond have had adventures on board submarines, while The Beatles' *Yellow Submarine* (1968) and Disney's *Atlantis* (2001) both included a colourful and action-packed submarine in their stories.

A LIFE OF LUXURY
If you have $78 million to spare, this personal submarine could be yours. *Phoenix 1000* is the world's first luxury submarine. She runs on the surface with diesel engines, dives on battery power, and resurfaces to recharge the batteries. It is possible to stay submerged for days. Designed to be as comfortable and safe as possible, personal submarines dive to about 300 m (980 ft).

SUBMARINE MUSEUM
Submarines such as USS *Bowfin* have been turned into popular museums. Built in 1943, USS *Bowfin* has long since stopped working, but is still in Hawaii where it was based in Pearl Harbour. Visitors can walk around and experience the boat as it was when it was in service. However, a clean submarine, without the engine smell and constant noise, would be a strange place to a crewman who had served on USS *Bowfin*.

Cramped crew quarters on USS *Bowfin*

Control planes

Propulsion motor

SUBMARINE RIDE
In the 1980s, the safest submarines in the world were to be found in Disneyland, California. The theme park ride allowed passengers to ride in the hull below the water and look out of the portholes. For safety reasons, the submarines never actually dived. As with many pleasure submarines, they were all yellow, like the one in The Beatles' film.

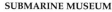

Viewing area for passengers

DIVER PROPULSION VEHICLE

Designed to save a diver time and energy, this torpedo-shaped vehicle can travel at speeds of up to 15 km/h (9 mph). Strong currents would hold back a diver swimming on their own, but a diver propulsion vehicle can get through fast–flowing waters without running into problems. This craft, pictured here in the Maldives, also enables the diver to stay underwater longer. The diver is using less energy, so breathes more slowly and uses up the air in the scuba tank less quickly.

TOURIST SUBMARINE

Over 40 tourist submarines have been constructed in the last ten years. Seven deep-dive vessels have also been adapted to carry passengers. Some tourist submarines can carry 64 people, and the electric-powered versions can dive to depths of up to 90 m (300 ft). Here, tourists are viewing shipwrecks from the *Mobilis* submarine in Saint-Pierre harbour, Martinique, in the Caribbean.

UNDERWATER HOTEL

Deep-sea workplaces for divers were first set up by Jacques Cousteau. Now there are underwater hotels for people wanting peace and quiet on holiday. This guest staying at the Jules Undersea Lodge in Key Largo off Florida is enjoying the view from his room.

Forward control room

Subs of the future

THE SUBMARINE WILL CONTINUE to play an important part in the 21st century. Wealthy nations will build and maintain nuclear submarines, while others will update their standard diesel-electric versions. A top priority for engineers and designers will be to develop new methods to power submarines. More deep-sea exploration will take place as more artefacts and minerals are brought to the surface. From the tiny "submarine" that could soon be visiting the inside of the human body, to large research submarines that may head out to explore the seas of other worlds, the range of tasks for submarines to tackle will be wider than ever before.

VISIONS OF THE FUTURE
The Victorians imagined using the submarine as underwater transport, following various routes, with one early proposal to shuttle passengers across the English Channel. In fact, many of their 19th-century dreams and ideas have now become reality as science has caught up with concepts.

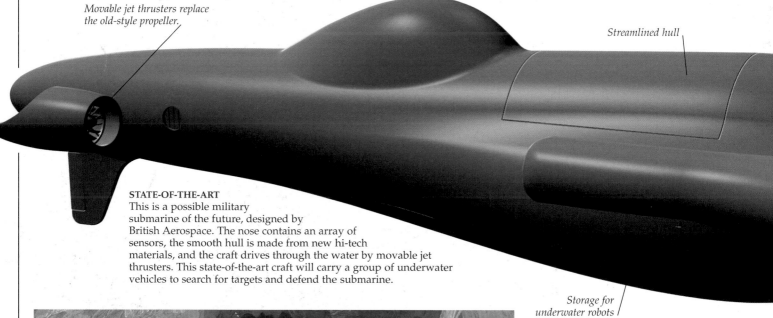

Movable jet thrusters replace the old-style propeller.

Streamlined hull

STATE-OF-THE-ART
This is a possible military submarine of the future, designed by British Aerospace. The nose contains an array of sensors, the smooth hull is made from new hi-tech materials, and the craft drives through the water by movable jet thrusters. This state-of-the-art craft will carry a group of underwater vehicles to search for targets and defend the submarine.

Storage for underwater robots

"Knowledge of the oceans is more than a matter of curiosity. Our very survival may hinge upon it."

US PRESIDENT JOHN F. KENNEDY
Message to Congress, March 1961

SUBMARINES IN SPACE
This is an artist's impression of a future NASA mission involving a submarine on one of the moons of the planet Jupiter. Scientists want to investigate whether there is an ocean under the surface of this moon. They plan to explore the surface layer using a remotely controlled submarine called a hydrobot. If this is successful, a hydrobot will be used to explore other planets with large areas of water.

DEEP FLIGHT

LOW FLYING
A new class of water-propelled submarine called Deep Flight has arrived. Priced at $10 million and designed by Graham Hawkes, it is lightweight and high-powered. Just under 4 m (12 ft) long, Deep Flight has room for one person to lie along the bottom of the cabin. A plastic nose cone gives all round vision. Deep Flight has such efficient steering that it can "fly" underwater and roll upside-down like a dolphin.

Deep Flight is the same shape as a mini space shuttle.

UNDERWATER LABORATORY
The Aquarius project is an American underwater laboratory working to protect the world's coral reefs. The laboratory is on a sandy lagoon close to the deep coral reefs of Florida Keys. Six scientists can stay for as long as ten days. Designed to withstand the pressure of depths up to 37 m (120 ft), the scientists enjoy a large living and working space with six bunkbeds, a shower, toilet, microwave, and fridge.

MODULAR TECHNOLOGY
The modern Virginia-Class nuclear submarine has a variety of sections that can be lifted out, modified, or replaced according to the needs of the vessel. Future submarines may be adapted like this, so new technologies can easily be added.

FANTASTIC VOYAGE
The next step in medical development will be investigations by a tiny submarine. In 1966, the science-fiction writer Isaac Asimov drew the nanoscale submarine shown here and called it "Fantastic Voyage". The hope is that one day the nanoscale submarine will be able to move through the human bloodstream, destroying diseased cells on the way.

Index

Acknowledgements

Dorling Kindersley would like to thank: Leah Germann, Steve Savage, Ben Hoare, Jo Connor.

The publishers would like to thank the following for their kind permission to reproduce their photographs:
a=above; b=below; c=centre; l=left; r=right; t=top

**Art Directors & Eyewitness Submarine Picture Credits
Agence France Presse:** 30crb; **AKG London:** 18tl, 18-19; British Library 12tr; U-Boat U53 Sinking a British Steamer by Claus Friedrich Bergen © DACS 2003 18tr; **Bovington Tank Museum:** 2tl; **Tim Brown:** 9cra, 15t, 22-23, 28-29, 28-29, 29cra, 29cr, 39tr, 43, 44cbl, 52cl, 52tcrr, 62-63; Corbis: 23tr, 25tr, 38cl, 42b; Bettmann 22tl, 27cr, 28c, 47crb, 50tr, 51cl, 51cla, 56tl; Jonathan Blair 59cr; Horace Bristol 41tl; Philip James Corwin 60bc; Bob Duff 41r;

Stephen Frink 61cr; JO1 Joe Gawlowicz 41cl; General Dynamics Electric Boat Division 11br; Philip Gould 61ca; George Hall 43tr; Hulton-Deutsch Collection 10bc, 35tl, 47c; WO Jack January 22-23; Steve Kaufman 30l, 31tl, 33b, 36bc, 40br; Larry Lee Photography 58crb; The Mariners' Museum 19tr, 42cla; Joe Marquette / Bettmann 54cra; Chris McLaughlin 57tc; PH1 Robert McRoy 41tl; PHC(DV) Mark Reinhard 6-7; Roger Ressmeyer 7bc, 36cl, 36-37, 49cl; Paul A. Sounders 59tl; Stocktrek 26l; Peter Turnley 29br; United States Navy 26-27; Ralph White 7tr, 52cl, 52cr, 53bl, 53tcl, 55tr; Yogi, Inc. 31tr, 39b; **Courtesy of the Department of National Defence/ Canadian Forces:** 37tc; **Mary Evans Picture Library:** 13tr, 16tr, 50bl, 54tl, 62tl; **Eyevine Ltd:** Corona Films / Zed / Saola 37c, 37br, 48br; **Global Marine Systems Limited:** From the archives of Global Marine Systems Limited 59b; **Frank Goddio:** Hilti Foundation / Christoph Gerigk 54-55b; **Ronald Grant Archive:** Paramount Pictures

60cal; **Hawkes Ocean Technologies/ www.deepflight.com:** 63t; **Ric Hedman TN(SS):** 20cl; **Imperial War Museum:** 18cl, 42cra; **Itar-tass Photo Agency:** Semyon Maisterman 46-47; **JAMSTEC:** 53c; **Kobal Collection:** Bavaria/Radiant 60tl; **David L. Mearns / Blue Water Recoveries Ltd:** 55c, 55cr; **NASA:** 62bl; **The Natural History Museum, London:** 56tr; **Naval Historical Foundation:** 20tr; N.H.P.A.: Ernie Janes 48car; Norbert Wu 53tcr, 56cl, 56cb, 56bl, 56br, 57cr, 57clb, 57crb, 57bl; **NOAA:** Courtesy of NOAA's Undersea Research Center at the University of North Carolina at Wilmington 63ca; Hawaii Undersea Research Laboratory, University of Hawaii 55br; OAR/Nationalk Undersea Research Program; JAMSTEC 53tc; R. Wicklund/OAR/ National Undersea Research Program (NURP) 58bl; **Novosti (London):** 27cl; **Oxford Scientific Films:** Paulo De Oliveira 56cla; **Popperfoto:** 6bl, 12crb; Reuters 41ca; **Rex Features:** Nils Jorgensen 55tl, 55cl, 55cbl; The **Royal Navy Submarine Museum:** 6tr, 8-9, 9cl, 9crb, 10cl, 11cr, 12c, 12-13, 13tl, 13cl, 15tr, 15cl, 15br, 16clb, 17cl, 17c, 17t, 19cl, 21cr, 21t, 23crb,

24c, 24b, 25clb, 26ca, 28cal, 28l, 31br, 32tl, 34tl, 34cr, 34crb, 35br, 38tr, 40tl, 40c, 41clb, 41bc, 43tl, 44tl, 44cl, 45c, 46tl, 46bl, 47tr, 47br, 48cl, 48cr, 49bl, 49r, 52tl; **Royal Tropical Institute:** 52tc; **Science Photo Library:** ESA / CE / Eurocontrol 45tc; W. Haxby, Lamont-Doherty Earth Observatory 45bc; Coneyl Jay 63br; Dr Ken Macdonald 45bcl; B. Murton/ Southampton Oceanography Centre 57br; Alexis Rosenfeld 7cr, 61tr; F.S. Westmorland 52-53; **TRH Pictures:** 19tl; Associated Press 24ca; **Courtesy of US Navy:** 28bl; **Courtesy of U.S. Air Force:** 28bl; **Courtesy of US Navy:** John E. Gay 44-45; US **Navy Submarine Force Museum, Groton:** 14bl, 22bl, 25ca, 25b; **U.S. Submarines Inc.:** 60-61; **VideoRay LLC:** With permission of VideoRay LLC - www.videoray.com 59c, 59cr.

All other images © Dorling Kindersley
For further information see:
www.dkimages.com